Minna no Nihongo

みんなの日本語

Intermediate Level I

中級Ⅰ 翻訳・文法解説 英語版

Translation & Grammatical Notes

スリーエーネットワーク

Published by 3A Corporation.
Trusty Kojimachi Bldg., 2F, 4, Kojimachi 3-Chome, Chiyoda-ku, Tokyo 102-0083, Japan

ISBN 978-4-88319-492-6 C0081

First published 2009
Printed in Japan

Foreword

Minna no Nihongo Chukyu (Japanese for Everyone – Intermediate) has been planned and edited to form a comprehensive set of Japanese-language learning materials following on from ***Minna no Nihongo Shokyu I*** and ***II*** (Japanese for Everyone – Introductory I & II), which were first published in 1998. The ***Minna no Nihongo Shokyu*** materials were originally developed to enable general adult beginners to acquire an introductory level of Japanese-language ability rapidly, but they are also widely used as introductory textbooks both in Japan and abroad by non-Japanese students either already studying at Japanese universities and colleges or preparing to do so.

Meanwhile, the number of non-Japanese intending to work in Japan or already living here continues to increase as the Japanese birthrate falls and international interchange gains pace, and the ***Minna no Nihongo*** books are also popular among such people because of the way the materials help them to learn Japanese easily.

As the range of people using the ***Minna no Nihongo*** books widened and demand for them increased, we began to receive requests from many different quarters for a set of intermediate materials that would follow on from ***Minna no Nihongo Shokyu I*** and ***II***. After extensive writing, testing and editing, we are now finally able to present everyone with what they have been asking for — ***Minna no Nihongo Chukyu***.

At the introductory level, people who need to communicate in Japanese are required to be able to say what they want to say and understand what is said to them. At the intermediate level, however, I believe they need more than this — they also need sufficiently good language skills to be able to understand and explore Japanese culture and customs. This book is designed to give ample support to learners like these.

Finally, I should like to thank everyone sincerely for their valuable opinions and for all the help they gave us in preparing and testing these materials. We at 3A Corporation intend to continue contributing to people's networking through activities such as developing and publishing the educational materials that today's multicultural, interdependent community requires, and I sincerely hope that you will continue to support and encourage us in this.

October 2008
Michihiro Takai
Chairman, 3A Corporation

Explanatory Notes

I. Structure of the Materials

The ***Minna no Nihongo Chukyu I*** materials consist of a Main Text (with CD) and the associated Translation and Grammar Notes (to be made available separately in various languages, starting with an English version). The materials aim to help learners develop a comprehensive set of Japanese-language skills in speaking/listening and reading/writing at the lower Intermediate level (enabling them to progress from introductory to intermediate level Japanese). ***Minna no Nihongo Chukyu I*** will be followed by ***Minna no Nihongo Chukyu II***, which will enable learners to develop their skills further and ultimately achieve a mastery of intermediate-level Japanese.

II. Contents and Method of Use

1. Main Text (with CD)

(1) Lessons

Minna no Nihongo Chukyu I contains twelve lessons and follows on from ***Minna no Nihongo Shokyu I*** and ***II*** (which contained a total of fifty lessons). They consist of:

1) Grammar and Practice Drills

The grammar points introduced in each lesson are presented in the form of sentence patterns. Grammar terminology is avoided.

When a sentence is connected to a sentence pattern, it is indicated by「…」,

e.g.「…ということだ」(Lesson 2).

When a noun or noun phrase is connected to a sentence pattern, it is indicated by「～」,

e.g.「～を～と言(い)う」(Lesson 1).

However, even if a connection is a sentence, it is indicated by「～」if its ending requires a special form such as the て-form, the た-form, the dictionary form, the たら-form, the ている-form, or the ば-form,

e.g.「～たら、～た」(Lesson 2).

The ways in which the grammar points (sentence patterns) are actually used are illustrated by example sentences and dialogues. Practice drills are provided to help learners develop their ability to use the grammar points, and illustrations are given whenever necessary to show the context. Learners are encouraged to make their own statements based on the sentence-pattern drills, which are designed to develop conversational topics and thereby strengthen conversational and reading comprehension skills.

2) Speak and Listen

Communication scenes are set out (mainly discussions and negotiations about everyday topics), and model dialogues and graded exercises (described below) are provided. By working through these exercises, which are designed to stimulate interest and increase learning motivation, learners ultimately become able to use the intended dialogues without relying on rote memorization. The characters appearing in the dialogues (old friends from ***Minna no Nihongo Shokyu I*** and ***II***) converse in a variety of situations.

1. やってみましょう (Let's Try It)
   This introduces the target dialogue. Learners use the Japanese they already know to make conversation in the situation described, in accordance with the set tasks.
2. 聞いてみましょう (Let's Listen)
   Learners listen to the dialogue on the CD, paying close attention to the key listening points and expressions introduced in each lesson.
3. もう一度聞きましょう (Let's Listen Again)
   Learners complete their comprehension of the dialogue by filling in the blanks in the exercises while listening to the dialogue on the CD again (playing it back in a way that matches their level of understanding of the material).
4. 言ってみましょう (Let's Try Saying It)
   Learners try repeating the dialogue as it is on the CD, focusing on their pronunciation and intonation.
5. 練習をしましょう (Let's Practice)
   Learners practice the words and expressions used in the dialogue.
6. 会話をしましょう (Let's Talk)
   Learners practice the dialogue by recreating it while looking at the illustrations.
7. チャレンジしましょう (Let's Challenge Ourselves)
   After understanding the situation and relationships described, learners practice the negotiation dialogue targeted in the lesson.

3) Read and Write

In「読みましょう」('Let's Read'), twelve different reading texts selected to pique readers' interest and enable them to enjoy reading have been provided.

1. 考えてみましょう (Let's Think About It)
   To prepare themselves to read the text, learners activate their knowledge of the topic.
2. ことばをチェックしましょう (Let's Check the Words)
   Learners do this exercise to make sure they know the key words (including new vocabulary) that they need in order to understand the text. They should check the meaning of any words they do not know in the new vocabulary list or a dictionary.

3. 読みましょう (Let's Read)

Each lesson's reading text is accompanied by「読むときのポイント」(Points to Note When Reading), which sets tasks designed to have learners practice the skills and strategies they need in order to understand the text. The aim is to enable them to obtain an accurate understanding of the gist of the text rapidly.

A text can be read silently or aloud, but the latter is also considered important here, and the CD contains specific examples of vocalized expressions for this purpose.

4. 答えましょう (Let's Answer)

Learners do this exercise to check whether they have correctly accomplished the tasks set in 'Points to Note When Reading.' Where necessary, there are also questions on the detailed contents of the texts.

5. チャレンジしましょう (Let's Challenge Ourselves)

The aim of this exercise is to enable learners to speak or write about their own experiences or familiar events relating to the contents of the reading text.

4) Revision Exercises

The Revision Exercises include ones for listening comprehension (indicated by the CD symbol), grammar, and vocabulary. The listening comprehension ones are of two types: listening to the CD and answering short questions, and listening to a short dialogue and grasping its key points. Both of these apply the key learning points introduced in the lesson and are designed to reinforce learners' listening comprehension. The grammar exercises check learners' understanding of the new sentence patterns introduced in each lesson, and the vocabulary exercises focus on enabling learners to remember and apply functional words.

(2) Key Learning Points

1) Speak and Listen

① Title of dialogue

② Learning goals (strategy)

③ Grammar points (sentence patterns) introduced in Speak and Listen (42 points)

④ ＊: Supplementary points (9 in total; see Explanatory Notes 2. Translation and Grammatical Notes)

2) Read and Write

① Title of reading text

② Hints for reading (strategy)

③ Grammar points (sentence patterns) introduced in Read and Write (53 points)

④ ＊: Supplementary points (8 in total; see Explanatory Notes 2. Translation and Grammatical Notes)

(3) Kanji Usage

1) As a rule, kanji are selected from the 常用漢字表 (the official list of kanji in common use) and its Appendix.

   ① 熟字訓 (kanji compounds having a special reading) that appear in the Appendix are written in kanji:

   e.g. 友達 friend　眼鏡 spectacles　二十歳 twenty years old　風邪 cold

   ② Proper nouns, and artistic, cultural and family-member names, are written in their own kanji even if those kanji do not appear in the official list:

   e.g. 厳島神社 Itsukushima Shrine
   夏目漱石 Natsume Soseki
   姪 niece

2) Some words are written in kana to simplify students' reading, even when their kanji are in the official list or its Appendix:

   e.g. ある（有る・在る）be
   いまさら（今更）now
   さまざま（様々）various

3) Numbers are chiefly shown in Arabic numerals:

   e.g. 9時 9 o'clock
   10月2日 2 October
   90歳 90 years old

   But kanji are used in cases like the following:

   e.g. 一人で by oneself
   一戸建て detached house
   一日中 all day long

4) The readings of all the kanji appearing in the Main Text of ***Minna no Nihongo Chukyu I*** are given in furigana.

(4) Indexes

1) New Vocabulary (approx. 910 words)
2) Conversational Expressions (approx. 50)
3) Kanji (315 of the official-list kanji appearing in the reading texts in all 12 lessons; introductory-level kanji omitted)

(5) Answers

1) Answers

   ① Grammar and Practice Drills, Speak and Listen, Read and Write

   ② Revision Exercises (including scripts for listening comprehension exercises)

   Some of the questions will have more than one possible answer, depending on the learner's background. The answers given here are merely model examples.

2) 'Speak and Listen' dialogue scripts

3) Contents of CD

(6) CD

The CD contains ① the dialogues from Speak and Listen, ② the reading texts from Read and Write, and ③ the listening comprehension parts of the Revision Exercises.

In addition to studying the pronunciation word by word while paying attention to accent and intonation, learners can use the dialogues to accustom themselves to Japanese spoken at normal speed, as well as to develop their ability to understand the key points in the flow of a conversation and answer questions about it.

Also, when listening to the reading texts, they can enjoy hearing the richness of Japanese expressions, which vary with the genre of the writing. They should pay attention to how the different parts of the text are read, and what rhythm and tone variation are used.

Finally, by using the Revision Exercises to check what they have learned, students can organize their thoughts and develop an all-round ability to apply their knowledge when speaking and writing.

2. Translation and Grammatical Notes (available as separate volumes in various languages)

These cover lessons 1 through 12 and contain the following:

(1) New Vocabulary and Its Translation

New words, conversational expressions and proper nouns are given in the order they appear in the lessons.

(2) Grammatical Notes

1) Grammar Points

The grammar points (sentence patterns) in each lesson have been compiled from the grammar syllabus considered necessary for intermediate-level learners.

2) Grammar Explanations (in various languages)

Explanations of the grammar points have been kept to the minimum needed by learners. Example sentences are used to clarify their meaning and function and indicate when and in what actual situations they can be used.

3) Connections

In the Main Text, thought has been given to making the connections understandable without using technical grammar terminology, by presenting grammar points in the form of sentence patterns and illustrating them with example sentences.

In each language version of the Grammatical Notes, the forms of all the connections are shown, so that learners can check them for themselves. Grammar terminology is also used where necessary.

4) References and Supplementary Notes

A second language is acquired not just by building up sequentially from the introductory stage, but also by working in spiral fashion (combining new grammar with previously-studied grammar, so that material already learned can be repeated and reinforced). The References show points introduced in ***Minna no Nihongo Shokyu*** and other relevant points. The supplementary points (in the Key Learning Points at the end of the Main Text) list points which, while not appearing in the Grammar and Practice Drills sections of the Main Text, are nevertheless considered useful for learners to know.

How to Use This Textbook Effectively

These notes explain the key points that learners should bear in mind in order to make most effective use of the ***Minna no Nihongo Chukyu I Main Text*** (with CD) and the associated ***Translation and Grammatical Notes*** (available separately in various languages).

I. *Minna no Nihongo Chukyu I Main Text* (with CD)

1. Grammar and Practice Drills

For each grammar point, begin by looking at the example sentences to see in what circumstances and situations the relevant sentence patterns and expressions can be used. Also compare these with elementary sentence patterns and expressions that can be used to express similar things. Then check the connections, do the Practice Drills, and try using what you have learned in actual speaking, listening, reading and writing situations.

2. Speak and Listen (Dialogue)

First, do Exercise 1「やってみましょう」('Let's Try It'), trying to create a conversation using the Japanese you already know. Then do Exercise 2「聞いてみましょう」('Let's Listen'), listening to the dialogue on the CD while paying close attention to the wording. Then do Exercise 3「もう一度聞きましょう」('Let's Listen Again'), filling in the blanks while listening to the dialogue on the CD once more. Then do Exercise 4「言ってみましょう」('Let's Try Saying It'), speaking the dialogue out loud along with the CD while paying attention to your pronunciation and intonation. Then do Exercise 5「練習をしましょう」('Let's Practice'), further practicing the expressions from the dialogue. Finally, do Exercise 6「会話をしましょう」('Let's Talk'), making up a conversation based on the pictures.

If you practice like this, you will become able to make conversation naturally, without having to force yourself to learn, and you will easily be able to extend your skills by doing Exercise 7「チャレンジしましょう」('Let's Challenge Ourselves').

The dialogue scripts can be found in the「解答」(Answers) section at the end of the book.

3. Read and Write (Reading Text)

Before reading the text, please get ready. Do Exercise 1「考えてみましょう」(Let's Think About It'), thinking about the topic of the text and discussing it with your classmates and teacher. Then do Exercise 2「ことばをチェックしましょう」('Let's Check the Words'), reviewing the words that appear in the text and looking up any unfamiliar ones in a dictionary or in the New Vocabulary list in ***Minna no Nihongo Chukyu I Translation and Grammatical Notes*** (available separately in various languages).

Next, do Exercise 3「読みましょう」('Let's Read'), reading the text yourself. Follow the instructions in the「読むときのポイント」('Points to Note When Reading') box, as you will need these in order to understand the text.

Then do Exercise 4「答えましょう」('Let's Answer'), to check how well you have understood the text. Finally do Exercise 5「チャレンジしましょう」('Let's Challenge Ourselves'), putting the finishing touches to your reading comprehension by telling others what you know about or have experienced concerning the topic of the text, writing about it, and so on.

There is a Kanji Index at the end of the book which gives the 315 常用漢字表 kanji appearing in this book (not including elementary ones) in their order of appearance. This will be a useful resource for learning how to read and write kanji and studying their meanings and uses.

4. Revision Exercises

Do these Revision Exercises to ensure that you have properly understood the meanings and usage of the grammar points and vocabulary introduced in the lesson. The answers are at the end of the book.

5. CD (🔊 : CD symbol)

Each lesson on the CD contains ① the dialogues from Speak and Listen, ② the reading texts from Read and Write and ③ the listening comprehension parts of the Revision Exercises.

🔊 Dialogue: The speed of the dialogues increases little by little with each successive lesson. Use them to get used to Japanese spoken at natural speed, and to practice grasping the key points of the conversations.

🔊 Reading Text: As you listen to the CD, pay attention to the rhythm and tone, as well as to how each part of the text is read.

🔊 Revision Exercises: Check your listening comprehension by doing these exercises, which introduce different applications of what you have learned in the lesson.

II. *Minna no Nihongo Chukyu I Translation and Grammatical Notes* (available separately in various languages)

These consist of New Vocabulary and Grammatical Notes.

1. New Vocabulary

New vocabulary, conversational expressions and proper nouns are given in the order in which they appear in the lessons. Check how they are used in the Main Text, and develop your ability to use and apply them by repeatedly practicing them together with the approximately 2,000 terms introduced in the introductory books.

2. Grammatical Notes

These explain the grammar of the approximately 100 grammar points (sentence patterns) appearing in the 'Speak and Listen' (dialogue) and 'Read and Write' (reading text) sections of each lesson. Improve your ability to use these by studying their meaning and function and deepening your understanding of them in actual conversational situations or in the context of the reading texts.

The ***Minna no Nihongo Chukyu I*** text has been designed to help learners make a smooth and enjoyable transition from introductory-level to intermediate-level Japanese, with the four functions (speaking, listening, reading and writing) of words and expressions introduced in a balanced way. We hope that they will help learners to develop their Japanese-language abilities to the lower intermediate level and build a sound platform for their next step of progressing to the higher intermediate level.

Terms Used for Instruction

		課（か）
依頼（いらい）	request	7
引用（いんよう）	quoting	6
確認（かくにん）	asking for confirmation	5
過去の意志（かこのいし）	past volition	6
勧誘（かんゆう）	invitation	10
義務（ぎむ）	obligatory	6
経験（けいけん）	experience	11
継続（けいぞく）	ongoing action	11
経歴（けいれき）	record, history	11
結果（けっか）	result	1
結果の状態（けっかのじょうたい）	resultant state	11
原因（げんいん）	cause	8
限定（げんてい）	limit	6
根拠（こんきょ）	logical ground	1
指示（しじ）	instruction	7
事態の出現（じたいのしゅつげん）	advent of a condition	6
習慣（しゅうかん）	habit	11
手段（しゅだん）	means	11
状況からの判断（じょうきょうからのはんだん）	guess from a situation	1
条件（じょうけん）	conditional	9
推量（すいりょう）	conjecture	5
提案（ていあん）	suggestion	11
丁寧な依頼表現（ていねいないらいひょうげん）	polite request	1
伝聞（でんぶん）	reported speech	4
動作の列挙（どうさのれっきょ）	listing of actions	12
判断（はんだん）	guess	1

		課（か）
比較（ひかく）	comparison	9
否定の意志（ひていのいし）	negative intention	6
比喩（ひゆ）	simile	1
文脈指示（ぶんみゃくしじ）	contextual demonstrative	5
変化（へんか）	change	11
理由（りゆう）	reason	1
例示（れいじ）	illustration	1
移動動詞（いどうどうし）	motion verb	5
感情動詞（かんじょうどうし）	emotion verb	7
状態動詞（じょうたいどうし）	stative verb	9
複合動詞（ふくごうどうし）	compound verbs	10
疑問詞（ぎもんし）	interrogative	5
固有名詞（こゆうめいし）	person's name or other proper noun	1
格助詞（かくじょし）	case particle	4
終助詞（しゅうじょし）	sentence-final particle	7
助数詞（じょすうし）	counter	1
受身（うけみ）	passive	7
間接受身（かんせつうけみ）	indirect passive	12
使役受身（しえきうけみ）	causative-passive	4
意向形（いこうけい）	volitional form	5
中止形（ちゅうしけい）	suspended form	4
である体（たい）	である style	4
丁寧形（ていねいけい）	polite form	4

		課（か）
普通形（ふつうけい）	plain form	1
会話（かいわ）	conversational	5
文章（ぶんしょう）	written	5
仮定（かてい）	subjunctive	2
使役（しえき）	causative	4
感情使役（かんじょうしえき）	emotional causative	7
完了（かんりょう）	perfective	2
逆接（ぎゃくせつ）	adversative conjunction	1
反事実的用法（はんじじつてきようほう）	counterfactual usage	9
付帯状況（ふたいじょうきょう）	attendant circumstances	11
並列（へいれつ）	parataxis	11
名詞修飾（めいししゅうしょく）	noun modifier	8
語幹（ごかん）	stem	12
主題（しゅだい）	topic	6
節（せつ）	clause	5
尊敬語（そんけいご）	respectful	9
同格（どうかく）	apposition	4

Abbreviations

N	Noun（名詞）
A	Adjective（形容詞）
い A	い -adjective（い形容詞）
な A	な -adjective（な形容詞）
V	Verb（動詞）
Vi.	V 自動詞
Vt.	V 他動詞
V ます -form	V ます形
V dic.-form	V 辞書形
V ない -form	V ない形
V た -form	V た形
V て -form	V て形
S	Sentence（文）

Characters

マイク・ミラー／ Mike Miller
American,
employee of IMC

松本(まつもと)　正(ただし)／ Matsumoto Tadashi
Japanese,
department manager at IMC

佐藤(さとう)　けい子(こ)／ Sato Keiko
Japanese,
employee of IMC

中村(なかむら)　秋子(あきこ)／ Nakamura Akiko
Japanese,
sales section manager at IMC

山田(やまだ)　一郎(いちろう)／ Yamada Ichiro
Japanese,
employee of IMC

山田(やまだ)　友子(ともこ)／ Yamada Tomoko
Japanese,
bank clerk

ジョン・ワット／ John Watt
British,
lecturer at Sakura University

太郎(たろう)／ Taro
Japanese, schoolboy (8 yrs.),
son of Ichiro and Tomoko Yamada

タワポン／ Thawaphon
Thai,
student at Sakura University

森(もり)／ Mori
Japanese,
professor at Sakura University

イー・ジンジュ／ Lee Jin Ju
Korean,
researcher at AKC

広田(ひろた)／ Hirota
Japanese,
student at Sakura University

佐野(さの)／ Sano
Japanese,
housewife

野村(のむら)／ Nomura
Japanese,
housewife

ホセ・サントス／ Jose Santos
Brazilian,
employee of Brazil Air

マリア・サントス／ Maria Santos
Brazilian,
housewife

カリナ／ Karina
Indonesian,
student at Fuji University

テレサ／ Teresa
Brazilian, schoolgirl (9 yrs.),
daughter of Jose and Maria Santos

池田／ Ikeda
Japanese,
employee of Brazil Air

カール・シュミット／ Karl Schmidt
German,
engineer at Power Electric Company

クララ・シュミット／ Klara Schmidt
German,
teacher of German

ワン・シュエ／ Wang Xue
Chinese,
doctor at Kobe Hospital

ハンス／ Hans
German, schoolboy (12 yrs.),
son of Karl and Klara Schmidt

リンリン／ Lin Lin
Chinese,
niece of Wang Xue

渡辺　あけみ／ Watanabe Akemi
Japanese,
employee of Power Electric Company

＊ IMC（computer software company）

＊ AKC（アジア研究センター：Asia Research Institute）

Contents

Part 2 Grammatical Notes

Part 1

Vocabulary

Lesson 1

どのように		how
迷う［道に～］	まよう［みちに～］	lose [one's way]
先輩	せんぱい	senior (student, colleague, etc.)
まるで		just (as in 'X is just like Y')
明るい［性格が～］	あかるい［せいかくが～］	cheerful [personality]
父親	ちちおや	father (cf. 母親(ははおや)：mother)
湖	みずうみ	lake
目指す	めざす	aim at, have one's eye on
命	いのち	life
おせち料理	おせちりょうり	traditional Japanese food for the New Year
初詣で	はつもうで	traditional practice of visiting a shrine or temple during the New Year to pray for happiness
畳	たたみ	tatami mat (thick straw mat used for flooring in traditional Japanese rooms)
座布団	ざぶとん	square floor cushion for sitting or kneeling on
床	ゆか	floor
正座	せいざ	formal kneeling position, with buttocks on heels, body upright, and hands in lap
おじぎ		bow (greeting)
作家	さっか	writer, author
～中［留守～］	～ちゅう［るす～］	while [while out]
いっぱい		full, crowded
どんなに		however, no matter how
立派［な］	りっぱ［な］	wonderful, grand
欠点	けってん	failing, shortcoming
～過ぎ	～すぎ	past, after, gone
似合う	にあう	suit, look good in

それで		so, therefore
お礼	おれい	thanks, appreciation
ポイント		key point
内容	ないよう	contents
聞き取る	ききとる	comprehend by listening
表現	ひょうげん	expression
迷う［AかBか〜］	まよう	be unable to decide [between A and B]
部分	ぶぶん	part
市民	しみん	citizen
会館	かいかん	assembly hall
市民会館	しみんかいかん	community center
伝統的［な］	でんとうてき［な］	traditional
実際に	じっさいに	actually
そういう		that kind of
ふだん		ordinary, usual
何とか	なんとか	somehow or other
イントネーション		intonation
奨学金	しょうがくきん	scholarship, bursary
推薦状	すいせんじょう	reference, letter of recommendation
交流	こうりゅう	social interchange (cf. 交流(こうりゅう)パーティー：get-to-know-you party)
司会	しかい	presiding over (a meeting or social event)
目上	めうえ	superior, of higher status
断る	ことわる	refuse
引き受ける	ひきうける	accept
印象	いんしょう	impression
チェックする		check
［お］住まい	［お］すまい	residence
たたむ		fold
重ねる	かさねる	place one on top of the other
板張り	いたばり	wooden (floor, ceiling, etc.)
素足	すあし	without socks

使い分ける	つかいわける	use selectively
良さ	よさ	merit, good quality
読み取る	よみとる	understand by reading or scrutinizing
旅行者	りょこうしゃ	tourist, traveller
～者	～しゃ	-er (person)
最も	もっとも	most
非常に	ひじょうに	very, extremely
それほど		to that extent
代表する	だいひょうする	represent
全体	ぜんたい	whole
敷く	しく	lay (a tatami mat), lay out (a futon, floor cushions)
ちょうど		just (as in 'X is just like Y')
何枚も	なんまいも	many (flat objects)
つける［名前を～］	［なまえを～］	apply, give [a name to]
やまとことば		word of purely Japanese origin
動かす	うごかす	move
組み合わせる	くみあわせる	combine, join together
客間	きゃくま	drawing room, parlor
居間	いま	living room, sitting room
仕事部屋	しごとべや	workroom, study
ワラ		straw
イグサ		mat rush
呼吸する	こきゅうする	breathe
湿気	しっけ	moisture, dampness
取る［湿気を～］	とる［しっけを～］	remove [moisture]
快適［な］	かいてき［な］	comfortable
清潔［な］	せいけつ［な］	clean
本文	ほんぶん	main text
一戸建て	いっこだて	detached house
小学生	しょうがくせい	primary school student

日常生活	にちじょうせいかつ	daily life

あのう、〜ていただけないでしょうか。	Excuse me, but I wonder if you could possibly...?
	Asking a difficult-to-ask favor, while showing hesitation by starting with「あのう」['Excuse me....'].
何(なん)とかお願(ねが)いできないでしょうか。	Couldn't you please find some way to oblige me?
	Showing that, despite knowing your request is unreasonable, you really would like it to be granted.
うちでよければどうぞ。	If our house would be all right, then please come along.
お役(やく)に立(た)ててよかったです。	I'm glad I was able to help.
お預(あず)かりします。	We'll take care of it.

村上春樹(むらかみはるき)	Haruki Murakami：Author and translator. 1949–.
『ノルウェイの森(もり)』	*Norwegian Wood*：One of Haruki Murakami's best-known works, translated into many languages.
南太平洋(みなみたいへいよう)	South Pacific
トンガ王国(おうこく)	The Kingdom of Tonga
バオバブ	Baobab：A tree native to Africa.
マダガスカル	Madagascar
タタミゼ	Tatamisé(e)：A French word signifying a person who has adopted the Japanese lifestyle and culture.

Lesson 2

ふく［ガラスを～］		wipe [the (window) glass]
結果	けっか	result
外来語	がいらいご	loanword
守る［地球を～］	まもる［ちきゅうを～］	protect [the earth]
ソフトウェア		software
メール		e-mail
郵便	ゆうびん	(postal) mail
Ｅメール	イーメール	e-mail
栄養	えいよう	nutrition
カロリー		calorie
エコ		eco, concern for the environment
環境	かんきょう	environment
アポ		appointment
省エネ	しょうエネ	energy-saving
学習する	がくしゅうする	learn
記事	きじ	article (in a newspaper, magazine, etc.)
分ける［ごみを～］	わける	separate [rubbish]
うわさ		rumor
辺り	あたり	area
アドバイス		advice
事件	じけん	incident
奪う	うばう	take, snatch, steal
干す	ほす	dry
以外	いがい	apart from, except
つく［うそを～］		tell [a lie]
ロボット		robot
本物	ほんもの	real thing
飛ぶ［空を～］	とぶ［そらを～］	fly [in the sky]

オレンジ		orange
パジャマ		pajamas
四角い	しかくい	square (in shape)
腕	うで	arm
つける［腕に～］	［うでに～］	attach to, wear on [one's arm]
ふるさと		hometown
話しかける	はなしかける	speak to, address
不在連絡票	ふざいれんらくひょう	'attempted delivery' notice
～宅	～たく	home, residence
工事	こうじ	construction
休日	きゅうじつ	holiday, day off
断水	だんすい	interruption to water supply
リモコン		remote control
ロボコン		Robot Contest
苦手［な］	にがて［な］	weak point, something one is not good at
紛らわしい	まぎらわしい	confusing
正確［な］	せいかく［な］	accurate
バランス		balance
引く［線を～］	ひく［せんを～］	draw [a line]
筆者	ひっしゃ	writer/author (of a piece)
いまだに		even now
とんでもない		Nothing of the sort!
宇宙人	うちゅうじん	alien, extraterrestrial being
全く	まったく	entirely
別の	べつの	another, different
～自身	～じしん	oneself
友人	ゆうじん	friend
また		moreover
ライス		cooked rice served with a Western meal
アドレス		address, e-mail address
メールアドレス		e-mail address
プレゼン		presentation

アイデンティティ		identity
コンプライアンス		compliance
例えば	たとえば	for example
ポリシー		policy, principles
場合	ばあい	case, situation
%	パーセント	percent
普通に	ふつうに	usually
いまさら		at this (late) stage, after all this time
必要	ひつよう	necessity
なくてはならない		indispensable
取る ［バランスを～］	とる	achieve [a balance]
文章	ぶんしょう	essay, sentence
比べる	くらべる	compare

2

8

お忙（いそが）しいところ、……。	(I'm sorry) to disturb you....

Addressing someone, while giving regard to their situation.

それで……。	And....

Listening to what they say, and encouraging them to say more.

僕自身（ぼくじしん）もそうだけど、……。	The same goes for me too, though.
何（なに）が何（なん）だかわからない。	I don't know what's what.

Lesson 3

インタビューする		interview
担当する	たんとうする	be in charge of, be responsible for
アルバイト先	アルバイトさき	part-time workplace
～先	～さき	place
店長	てんちょう	store manager
研修	けんしゅう	training
話し合う	はなしあう	discuss
通勤する	つうきんする	commute
これまで		until now
減らす	へらす	reduce
引っ越す	ひっこす	move（house）
～か国	～かこく	（number of） countries
家庭	かてい	household, home, family
事情	じじょう	circumstances, reasons
幼稚園	ようちえん	kindergarten, preschool
昼寝する	ひるねする	have (take) a daytime nap
帰国する	きこくする	return to one's home country
来社	らいしゃ	come to visit (a company/office)
新製品	しんせいひん	new product
新～	しん～	new, novel
発表会	はっぴょうかい	presentation
いつまでも		indefinitely
景気	けいき	economy, business conditions
これ以上	これいじょう	any longer
森	もり	forest
声［市民の～］	こえ［しみんの～］	voice [of the people], opinion
受ける［インタビューを～］	うける	be interviewed, receive [an interview]
要望	ようぼう	request, wish

3

本当は	ほんとうは	really
おとなしい		gentle, quiet
しゃべる		talk
振る［彼女を～］	ふる［かのじょを～］	dump, jilt [a girlfriend]
Tシャツ	ティーシャツ	T-shirt
数	かず	number
切る［電話を～］	きる［でんわを～］	hang up [the phone]
秘書	ひしょ	secretary
教授	きょうじゅ	professor
わざわざ		specially, going to the trouble of
取る［時間を～］	とる［じかんを～］	set aside [time]
できれば		if possible
変更する	へんこうする	change
急用	きゅうよう	urgent business
気にする	きにする	be concerned about
取引先	とりひきさき	client, customer
学生用	がくせいよう	for use by students
～用［学生～］	～よう［がくせい～］	for use by [students]
コンピューター室	コンピューターしつ	computer room
～室	～しつ	～ room
渋滞	じゅうたい	(traffic) jam, holdup
瞬間	しゅんかん	instant, moment
意識	いしき	awareness, sense
アンケート		questionnaire
調査	ちょうさ	investigation, survey
傾向	けいこう	trend
避ける	さける	avoid
悲観的［な］	ひかんてき［な］	pessimistic
グラフ		graph
時	とき	time
最高に	さいこうに	most

もう一つ	もうひとつ	another, one more
あいだ		while
前者	ぜんしゃ	former
後者	こうしゃ	latter
やはり		after all
恋	こい	love
幸せ	しあわせ	happiness
感じる	かんじる	feel
寝坊する	ねぼうする	oversleep
危険	きけん	danger
寝顔	ねがお	face of a sleeping person

お電話（でんわ）、代（か）わりました。	Hello, [name] here.
どうかしましたか。	Is something the matter?
わざわざ～ていただいたのに、……。	After you went to the trouble of....

Letting someone know you are sorry for having made their kindness a wasted effort.

困（こま）りましたね。	Oh, dear.
できれば、～ていただけないでしょうか。	If possible, I wonder if we could....

Tactfully communicating a wish.

おいでください。	Please come.
申（もう）し訳（わけ）ありませんでした。	I'm very sorry.

東北（とうほく）　Tohoku：The Tohoku region of Japan, comprising the prefectures of Aomori, Iwate, Akita, Yamagata, Miyagi and Fukushima.

Lesson 4

検査する	けんさする	examine, inspect
明日	あす	tomorrow
能力	のうりょく	capability
バザー		bazaar
マスク		nose and mouth mask
スーツケース		suitcase
目が覚める	めがさめる	wake up, realize
朝礼	ちょうれい	morning meeting
校歌	こうか	school song
敬語	けいご	honorific language
感想文	かんそうぶん	review (e.g., of a book one has read)
運動場	うんどうじょう	sports ground
いたずら		prank
美しい	うつくしい	beautiful
世紀	せいき	century
平和［な］	へいわ［な］	peaceful
人々	ひとびと	people
願う	ねがう	desire, wish for, hope for
文	ぶん	sentence, style
書き換える	かきかえる	rewrite
合わせる	あわせる	combine
もともと		originally
若者	わかもの	young person
～湖	～こ	lake ～
深い	ふかい	deep
さまざま［な］		various
苦しい［生活が～］	くるしい［せいかつが～］	hard
性格	せいかく	character
人気者	にんきもの	popular person

多く	おおく	many
不安［な］	ふあん［な］	worried
出る［製品が～］	でる［せいひんが～］	[product] come on sale
雷	かみなり	thunder
うち		we, us (cf. うちの子ども：my children)
残念［な］	ざんねん［な］	disappointing, regrettable
認める	みとめる	accept
現実	げんじつ	fact, reality
愛する	あいする	love
首都	しゅと	capital (city)
伝言	でんごん	message
留守番電話	るすばんでんわ	answerphone, voicemail
メッセージ		message
受ける［伝言を～］	うける［でんごんを～］	receive [a message]
入れる［メッセージを～］	いれる	leave [a message]
差し上げる［電話を～］	さしあげる［でんわを～］	give [a call]
そのように		like that (cf. このように：like this)
出る［電話に～］	でる［でんわに～］	answer [the telephone]
急［な］	きゅう［な］	urgent
入る［仕事が～］	はいる［しごとが～］	[work] come in
取り消す	とりけす	cancel, erase
来客中	らいきゃくちゅう	with a visitor
食パン	しょくパン	bread
売り切れ	うりきれ	sold out
バーゲンセール		(bargain) sale
案内状	あんないじょう	(written) invitation
～状［招待～］	～じょう［しょうたい～］	letter, note, card [of invitation]
遠い［電話が～］	とおい［でんわが～］	faint, hard to hear [voice on telephone]
～嫌い	～ぎらい	dislike

4

時代	じだい	period, era, times
順に	じゅんに	in sequence
失礼［な］	しつれい［な］	rude
勧める	すすめる	recommend
腹を立てる	はらをたてる	get angry
味わう	あじわう	experience, taste
つなぐ		hold (hands), connect (lines)
エピソード		episode
大嫌い	だいきらい	hate
大～	だい～	greatly [like/dislike]
［好き／嫌い］	［すき／きらい］	
しつこい		persistent
全員	ぜんいん	everyone
数日	すうじつ	a few days
親せき	しんせき	relative
接続する	せつぞくする	connect
申し出る	もうしでる	offer, propose
結局	けっきょく	in the end
早速	さっそく	immediately
そば		beside
取り付ける	とりつける	install
出席者	しゅっせきしゃ	attendee
料金	りょうきん	fee, charge

いつもお世話(せわ)になっております。　We are much obliged to you.

あいにく……。　Unfortunately....

> Letting someone know you feel sorry for being unable to do what they had hoped you would do.

恐(おそ)れ入(い)りますが、……。　Excuse me for asking, but....

> A standard expression always used when asking a favor of someone to whom one has to show respect.

このままでよろしければ　If it is all right the way it is....

ただいまのメッセージをお預かりしました。	Your message has been recorded.
ごめん。	Sorry.

日本語能力試験	The Japanese Language Proficiency Test：A test for assessing and certifying the Japanese-language ability of non-native speakers of Japanese.
摩周湖	Lake Mashu：A lake in Hokkaido.
夏目漱石	Natsume Soseki：Novelist, critic, and English literature scholar. 1867–1916.
マーク・トゥエイン	Mark Twain：American author. 1835–1910.
H. G. ウェルズ	H. G. Wells：British author and critic. 1866–1946.
グラハム・ベル	Alexander Graham Bell：American physicist and inventor. Invented the telephone. 1847–1922.
ハートフォード	Hartford：City in Connecticut State, on the East Coast of America.

Lesson 5

教科書	きょうかしょ	textbook
居酒屋	いざかや	pub, tavern
やきとり		grilled chicken parts on skewers
画面	がめん	picture, screen
俳優	はいゆう	actor
そっくり		looking exactly like
コンビニ		convenience store
改札［口］	かいさつ［ぐち］	ticket [inspection] barrier
運転手	うんてんしゅ	driver
かかってくる		[telephone] ring
［電話が～］	［でんわが～］	
切れる［電話が～］	きれる［でんわが～］	[telephone] stop ringing, be cut off
挙げる［例を～］	あげる［れいを～］	give [an example]
未来	みらい	future
なくす［戦争を～］	［せんそうを～］	get rid of [war]
不思議［な］	ふしぎ［な］	strange, mysterious, wonderful
増やす	ふやす	increase
今ごろ	いまごろ	about now
観光客	かんこうきゃく	sightseer, tourist
沿う［川に～］	そう［かわに～］	～ along [a river]
大通り	おおどおり	main street, avenue
出る［大通りに～］	でる［おおどおりに～］	come out [on the main street]
横断歩道	おうだんほどう	pedestrian crossing
突き当たり	つきあたり	end (of a street)
線路	せんろ	railway line
向こう側	むこうがわ	far side
踏切	ふみきり	level crossing
分かれる	わかれる	[road] divide
［道が～］	［みちが～］	

芸術	げいじゅつ	art
道順	みちじゅん	way, route
通行人	つうこうにん	passer by
通り	とおり	street, road
川沿い	かわぞい	beside (along) a river
～沿い	～ぞい	along, beside
流れる	ながれる	flow
～先 ［100 メートル～］	～さき	[100 m] ahead
～方［右の～］	～ほう［みぎの～］	direction [to the right]
南北	なんぼく	north and south
逆	ぎゃく	opposite, reverse
南半球	みなみはんきゅう	Southern Hemisphere
北半球	きたはんきゅう	Northern Hemisphere
常識	じょうしき	customary behavior, common practice
差別	さべつ	discrimination
平等［な］	びょうどう［な］	equal
位置	いち	position, location
人間	にんげん	person, human being
観察する	かんさつする	observe
面	めん	surface
中央	ちゅうおう	center
自然に	しぜんに	naturally
努力する	どりょくする	try, make an effort
そこで		so
普通	ふつう	usually
経緯度	けいいど	latitude and longitude
無意識に	むいしきに	unconsciously
表れ	あらわれ	sign, manifestation
上下	じょうげ	top and bottom, up and down, vertically
左右	さゆう	left and right, laterally
少なくとも	すくなくとも	at least

文句	もんく	complaint
わざと		deliberately
経度	けいど	longitude
緯度	いど	latitude
使用する	しようする	use
東西	とうざい	East and West

～から、～てください。

> Describing a route by mentioning landmarks so that the listener clearly understands.

函館（はこだて）	Hakodate：Port city in the south of Hokkaido.
東京（とうきょう）タワー	Tokyo Tower：Television tower erected in Minato Ward, Tokyo, in 1958.
アラビア語（ご）	Arabic
マッカーサー	Stuart McArthur：Australian high-school teacher.
アフリカ	Africa
南（みなみ）アメリカ	South America

Lesson 6

一期一会	いちごいちえ	'Treasure each moment as a once-in-a-lifetime experience.'
フクロウ		owl
学ぶ	まなぶ	study, learn
一生	いっしょう	one's whole life
店員	てんいん	shop assistant
就職する	しゅうしょくする	get a job
自分では	じぶんでは	Personally,....
ゲーム		game
うがい		gargle
ビタミンC	ビタミンシー	vitamin C
とる［ビタミンを～］		take [a vitamin]
遠く	とおく	far off
太鼓	たいこ	drum
けいこ		training, practice, rehearsal
サケ		salmon
着陸する	ちゃくりくする	land (an aircraft lands)
振る［手を～］	ふる［てを～］	wave [one's hand]
タラップ		(movable) steps
ようこそ		welcome
ビジネスマナー		business etiquette
セミナー		seminar, workshop
案内	あんない	information, description
費用	ひよう	cost
交渉する	こうしょうする	negotiate
条件	じょうけん	conditions
制度	せいど	system

メンタル　トレーニング		mental training
取り入れる	とりいれる	include, incorporate, adopt
ビジネス		business
レベル		level
週	しゅう	week
全額	ぜんがく	full price
半額	はんがく	half price
出す［費用を～］	だす［ひようを～］	allow [an expense]
それでは		in that case
期間	きかん	period (of time)
日時	にちじ	date and time
授業料	じゅぎょうりょう	lesson fee
～料	～りょう	～ fee
日にち	ひにち	date (of a meeting, etc.)
担当者	たんとうしゃ	person in charge, coordinator
延期する	えんきする	postpone
買い換える	かいかえる	replace [by buying a new one]
講演会	こうえんかい	lecture
～会［講演～］	～かい［こうえん～］	[lecture] meeting
上司	じょうし	boss, person one reports to
つかむ		grasp
そのような		that kind of
想像する	そうぞうする	imagine
イメージする		visualize
具体的［な］	ぐたいてき［な］	specific, concrete
理想	りそう	ideal
近づく	ちかづく	approach
こそあど		demonstrative and interrogative words that begin with the syllables こ, そ, あ and ど
指す	さす	indicate, refer to
記者会見	きしゃかいけん	press conference

6

記者	きしゃ	reporter
会見	かいけん	interview
～ごっこ		playing at ～
キャベツ		cabbage
暗い［気持ちが～］	くらい［きもちが～］	gloomy
世の中	よのなか	the world
アホ		stupid, ridiculous
見える［アホに～］	みえる	appear/seem [stupid]
ビジネスマン		businessman
同じような	おなじような	same kind of
閉じる	とじる	close
トレーニング		training
つまり		that is to say, in other words
過去	かこ	past
向き合う	むきあう	face one another
そうすれば		if you do so, then, if so
現在	げんざい	present, now
そこから		from there
解決する	かいけつする	solve
プラン		plan
立てる［プランを～］	たてる	make [a plan]
順番	じゅんばん	order, sequence

いやあ、……。	No....
今(いま)ちょっとよろしいでしょうか。	Have you got a moment?
実(じつ)は～のことなんですが、……。	As a matter of fact, it's about....

An expression used for announcing what you want to talk about when negotiating or asking a favor.

ふうん。	Oh, really?

もし～が無理(むり)なら、……。　　If...is too much to ask....

Showing that one is prepared to negotiate, and proposing an alternative.

「ちょうちょ」	'Butterfly' : Nursery rhyme.
スバル	The Pleiades : Star cluster in the constellation of Taurus, visible to the naked eye.
日本留学試験(にほんりゅうがくしけん)	Examination for Japanese University Admission for International Students : Test of Japanese-language proficiency and basic academic ability for non-Japanese students wishing to enter a Japanese university.
羽田空港(はねだくうこう)	Haneda Airport : Airport in Ota Ward, Tokyo.

Lesson 7

出す［料理を～］	だす［りょうりを～］	serve [food]
歓迎会	かんげいかい	welcome party, reception
招待状	しょうたいじょう	(written) invitation
ラーメン		ramen (Chinese noodles in broth)
折り紙	おりがみ	origami (the art of paper folding)
ピンク		pink
送別会	そうべつかい	farewell party
中華レストラン	ちゅうかレストラン	Chinese restaurant
留学生会	りゅうがくせいかい	International Students' Association
～会	～かい	～ association
［留学生～］	［りゅうがくせい～］	[International Students' ～]
会長	かいちょう	chairperson
点数	てんすう	score
たいした		[no] big deal
悪口	わるぐち	badmouthing, derogatory remarks
夫婦	ふうふ	married couple
～げんか［夫婦～］	［ふうふ～］	quarrel [between husband and wife]
医学部	いがくぶ	medical faculty
～部［医学～］	～ぶ［いがく～］	[medical] faculty (department)
ライオン		lion
喜ぶ	よろこぶ	be pleased
冗談	じょうだん	joke
～たち［子ども～］	［こども～］	(plural suffix)
お化け	おばけ	ghost, specter
いじめる		bully
感心する	かんしんする	be impressed
親	おや	parent[s]
あらためて		again, afresh, anew
一周	いっしゅう	once around

7

～山	～さん	Mt. (e.g., Mt. Fuji)
芝居	しばい	play, show
せりふ		lines (in a play)
泣く	なく	cry (with emotion)
アニメ		cartoon film, animation
感動する	かんどうする	be moved by
講演	こうえん	lecture
譲る	ゆずる	hand over to
ツアー		tour
きつい［スケジュールが～］		tough [schedule, etc.]
フリーマーケット		flea market
遠慮する	えんりょする	decline
表す	あらわす	show
失礼	しつれい	impoliteness
受ける［誘いを～］	うける［さそいを～］	accept [an invitation]
着付け教室	きつけきょうしつ	class for learning how to put on and wear kimono correctly
待ち合わせる	まちあわせる	meet up
空く［時間が～］	あく［じかんが～］	be free [have some free time]
交流会	こうりゅうかい	get-to-know-you party
いろんな		various
ゼミ		seminar
せっかく		kindly
今回	こんかい	on this occasion
同僚	どうりょう	colleague
登山	とざん	mountain climbing
紅葉	こうよう	gorgeous autumn foliage
見物	けんぶつ	sightseeing, viewing
音楽会	おんがくかい	recital, concert
まんじゅう		bean-jam bun
ヘビ		snake

毛虫	けむし	caterpillar
いばる		throw one's weight around
震える	ふるえる	tremble, shiver
すると		thereupon
おれ		I, me (used by men)
～ぐらい		at least
お前	おまえ	you (used by men)
丸い	まるい	round
いや		no
震え出す	ふるえだす	begin to tremble
助ける	たすける	help, save
次々に	つぎつぎに	one after another
目の前	めのまえ	in front of one's eyes
ポツリと		mutteringly
ホームページ		website
笑い話	わらいばなし	funny story
落語	らくご	Rakugo (traditional Japanese comic storytelling)

本当(ほんとう)ですか。	Really?
ぜひお願(ねが)いします。	Oh, yes, please.

Gladly accepting an invitation.

せっかく誘(さそ)っていただいたのに、申(もう)し訳(わけ)ありません。今回(こんかい)は遠慮(えんりょ)させてください。	I really appreciate the invitation, but I'm afraid I'll have to decline this time.

Politely declining an invitation while expressing great regret.

……かい？	(suffix indicating a question)
助(たす)けてくれ！	Help!

Lesson 8

眠る	ねむる	sleep
黙る	だまる	remain silent
取る［ノートを～］	とる	take [notes]
盗む	ぬすむ	steal
焦げる	こげる	burn, get scorched
枯れる	かれる	wither, dry up
平凡［な］	へいぼん［な］	commonplace
人生	じんせい	life
免許	めんきょ	license
取る［免許を～］	とる［めんきょを～］	get [a license]
退職する	たいしょくする	retire
もったいない		wasteful
鍋	なべ	pot
ことば遣い	ことばづかい	use of language, way of talking
生	なま	raw
専門的［な］	せんもんてき［な］	specialized
社会勉強	しゃかいべんきょう	learning about the world
高校生	こうこうせい	high-school student
迷子	まいご	lost child, getting lost
しま		stripe
花柄	はながら	floral pattern
チェック		check
スカート		skirt
無地	むじ	unpatterned
水玉	みずたま	polka dots
リュック		rucksack, backpack
背負う	せおう	carry on one's back
サービスカウンター		service counter
姪	めい	niece

特徴	とくちょう	characteristic, feature
身長	しんちょう	height
ジーンズ		jeans
髪型	かみがた	hairstyle
肩	かた	shoulder
持ち物	もちもの	personal belongings
水色	みずいろ	pale blue
折りたたみ	おりたたみ	folding
青地	あおじ	blue background
～地	～じ	background
持つところ	もつところ	handle
プラスチック		plastic
途上国	とじょうこく	developing country
先進国	せんしんこく	developed country
プラス		advantage
マイナス		disadvantage
共通	きょうつう	common
関心	かんしん	interest
多様化	たようか	diversification
タイトル		title
反対に	はんたいに	conversely
前後	ぜんご	the front and the back
対象	たいしょう	subject
少女	しょうじょ	young girl
アイディア		idea
輝く	かがやく	beam, dazzle, sparkle, brilliant
浮力	ふりょく	buoyancy
少年	しょうねん	boy
キノコ雲	キノコぐも	mushroom cloud
時に	ときに	sometimes
ダメージ		damage

与える ［ダメージを～］	あたえる	cause [damage]
ひげ		beard
伸びる	のびる	grow
発展する	はってんする	develop
ページ		page
魅力	みりょく	attractiveness
豊か［な］	ゆたか［な］	affluent
受ける ［ダメージを～］	うける	receive, sustain [damage]
テーマ		topic
述べる	のべる	state, speak

8

確(たし)か、～たと思(おも)います。 I'm pretty sure... was....

Explaining something while recollecting someone's appearance or memory.

ナイジェリア	Nigeria
トリニダードトバゴ	Trinidad and Tobago
インド	India
ウガンダ	Uganda

Lesson 9

決まる	きまる	be decided
済む	すむ	be over
印鑑	いんかん	stamp, (personal/official) seal
サイン		signature
性能	せいのう	performance
タイプ		type
機能	きのう	function
平日	へいじつ	weekday
将棋	しょうぎ	shogi (Japanese board game resembling chess)
自慢する	じまんする	feel proud of, boast about
豚肉	ぶたにく	pork
牛肉	ぎゅうにく	beef
バレーボール		volleyball
気温	きおん	(atmospheric) temperature
降水量	こうすいりょう	(amount of) rainfall
月別	つきべつ	month by month
平均	へいきん	average
予防注射	よぼうちゅうしゃ	vaccination
国々	くにぐに	countries
都市	とし	city
入国する	にゅうこくする	enter a country
資源	しげん	(natural) resources
とれる［米が～］	［こめが～］	[rice] be grown/be harvested
大雪	おおゆき	heavy snowfall
乾燥する	かんそうする	dry out
道路	どうろ	road
どんどん		rapidly
最後	さいご	end

生きる	いきる	live
誕生	たんじょう	birth
実現する	じつげんする	become a reality
金メダル	きんメダル	gold medal
金	きん	gold
メダル		medal
バスケットボール		basketball
選手	せんしゅ	player, athlete
シンプル［な］		simple
書き込み	かきこみ	writing
検索	けんさく	retrieval
例文	れいぶん	example sentence
ジャンプ機能	ジャンプきのう	'jump function' or 'skip-search' of electronic dictionaries
ジャンプ		jump
商品	しょうひん	product, commodity, merchandise
～社	～しゃ	Co.
国語辞書	こくごじしょ	Japanese dictionary
和英辞書	わえいじしょ	Japanese-English dictionary
載る［例文が～］	のる［れいぶんが～］	[examples] be given
シルバー		silver
付け加える	つけくわえる	add to
編集する	へんしゅうする	edit
しっかり		reliably, properly
留守番をする	るすばんをする	stay and look after [a house] while everyone else is out
柄	がら	pattern
共通語	きょうつうご	common language
演奏	えんそう	performance
特許	とっきょ	patent
倒産	とうさん	bankruptcy, insolvency
大金持ち	おおがねもち	millionaire

誇る	ほこる	be proud of
表れる	あらわれる	be revealed in
今では	いまでは	now, today
ＴＳＵＮＡＭＩ	ツナミ	tsunami, seismic sea wave
影響	えいきょう	influence
有名人	ゆうめいじん	famous person
録音する	ろくおんする	record
ヒント		hint
貸し出す	かしだす	rent out
ところが		however
競争	きょうそう	competition
性別	せいべつ	sex, gender
地域	ちいき	region
関係なく	かんけいなく	regardless of
娯楽	ごらく	amusement, recreation
［お］年寄り	［お］としより	elderly person
仲間	なかま	friend
心	こころ	mind
治す	なおす	cure
単なる	たんなる	mere
きっかけ		reason, catalyst
交流協会	こうりゅうきょうかい	exchange association
広報誌	こうほうし	public relations magazine, bulletin
暮らし	くらし	life
役立つ	やくだつ	be useful for
参加者	さんかしゃ	participant

こうやって	Like this....
～だけじゃなくて、～のがいいんですが……。	Not just..., but... would be good.

Adding desired conditions regarding something one wants to buy.

それでしたら、～（の）がよろしいんじゃないでしょうか。	In that case, would'nt ～ be best?
ほとんど変(か)わりませんね。	There's hardly any difference.
～で、～はありませんか。	Do you have... with... ?

Asking for an article that is of a different type to, but satisfies the same conditions as, the one suggested by the shop assistant.

ドラえもん	*Doraemon*：Robot-cat hero of manga and anime series, translated into many languages and popular world-wide.
アインシュタイン	Albert Einstein：German (American naturalized) theoretical physicist and Nobel Prize winner. 1879–1955.
タイム	*Time*：American weekly news magazine, published in thirty countries.
ガンジー	Gandhi：Mohandas Karamchand Gandhi, Indian politician and thinker. 1869–1948.
毛沢東(もうたくとう)	Mao Zedong：Chinese politician and thinker, founder of the People's Republic of China. 1893–1976.
黒澤明(くろさわあきら)	Akira Kurosawa：Film director, best known for 'The Seven Samurai.' 1910–1998.
井上大佑(いのうえだいすけ)	Daisuke Inoue：Inventor of karaoke. 1949–.
8(エイト)ジューク	8-track jukebox：The first karaoke device, invented by Daisuke Inoue in 1971.
曲(ま)がるストロー	bendy straw：Invented and patented by Takao Sakata after seeing a friend in hospital having difficulty drinking through a straight straw.
プルトップリング	ring pull：Ring-shaped tab for opening a drinking hole in the lid of a drink can.

Lesson 10

もうける		make [money], earn
［お金を～］	［おかねを～］	
見かける	みかける	notice, catch sight of
否定する	ひていする	deny
タイムマシン		time machine
宝くじ	たからくじ	lottery
当たる	あたる	win [a lottery]
［宝くじが～］	［たからくじが～］	
ワールドカップ		World Cup
カエル		frog
計画	けいかく	plan
実際	じっさい	actuality
めったに		seldom
通じる	つうじる	get through [on the telephone]
［電話が～］	［でんわが～］	
時間通りに	じかんどおりに	on time
かかる		[engine] start
［エンジンが～］		
鬼	おに	demon
怒る	おこる	get angry
CO_2	シーオーツー	CO_2
抽選	ちゅうせん	draw, ballot
一等	いっとう	first place
投票	とうひょう	voting
［お］互いに	［お］たがいに	each other
出す［修理に～］	だす［しゅうりに～］	send [for repair]
聞き返す	ききかえす	ask to have something explained again
てっきり		definitely
倉庫	そうこ	storeroom, warehouse

プリンター		printer
入る［電源が～］	はいる［でんげんが～］	[power] be on
マニュアル		manual
親しい	したしい	close, familiar
驚く	おどろく	be surprised
～代［60～］	～だい	-ies［sixties］
誤解	ごかい	misunderstanding
記憶	きおく	memory
型	かた	type
～型	～がた	～ type
落とし物	おとしもの	lost property
転ぶ	ころぶ	fall over
奇数	きすう	odd number
偶数	ぐうすう	even number
ぼんやりする		daydream, woolgather
あわて者	あわてもの	careless person
ミス		mistake
これら		these
ヒューマンエラー		human error
手術	しゅじゅつ	operation
患者	かんじゃ	patient
心理学者	しんりがくしゃ	psychologist
おかす［ミスを～］		make [a mistake]
うっかりミス		careless mistake
うっかり		careless
こういう		this kind of, such (cf. ああいう：that kind of)
チェックリスト		checklist
手がかり	てがかり	hint, clue
一方	いっぽう	on the other hand
深く［～呼吸する］	ふかく［～こきゅうする］	[breathe] deeply

指	ゆび	finger
聖人君子	せいじんくんし	model of all virtues
うそつき		liar
または		or
エラー		error
困った人	こまったひと	hopeless person
完成する	かんせいする	complete
つながる		lead to [an incident]
［出来事に～］	［できごとに～］	
出来事	できごと	incident
不注意	ふちゅうい	carelessness
引き起こす	ひきおこす	cause, bring about

どういうことでしょうか。 — What are you talking about?

> Expressing the feeling that you are nonplussed by what you have just been told.

そんなはずはありません。 — That can't be true!

てっきり～と思(おも)っていました。 — I was sure that....

> Telling the listener what you have believed up till now, and expressing the feeling that you find it hard to believe what you have just heard.

気(き)を悪(わる)くする — get upset

わかってもらえればいいんです。 — I'm happy if you understand.

ＪＲ　JR : Abbreviation for Japan Railways.

沖縄県(おきなわけん)　Okinawa Prefecture : The southernmost Japanese prefecture, comprising the main island of Okinawa, the Ryukyu Islands and other islands. The Okinawa Prefectural Office is located in the city of Naha.

マザー・テレサ	Mother Teresa：Albanian Roman Catholic nun renowned for her missionary work in India. Nobel Prize winner. 1910–1997.
新宿(しんじゅく)	Shinjuku：One of Tokyo's subcenters. The Tokyo Metropolitan Government Office relocated there in 1991.
リーズン	James Reason：British psychologist. Books include *Human Error* and *Managing the Risks of Organizational Accidents*.

10

Lesson 11

ますます		more and more
企業	きぎょう	business enterprise
今後	こんご	from now on
方言	ほうげん	dialect
普及する	ふきゅうする	become widespread
建つ	たつ	be built
大家族	だいかぞく	large family
大～［～家族］	だい～［～かぞく］	large [family]
パックツアー		package tour
個人	こじん	individual
いかにも		so, really, certainly, indeed, very
入学式	にゅうがくしき	(school/college) entrance ceremony
派手［な］	はで［な］	flamboyant
元気	げんき	vitality, cheerfulness
出す［元気を～］	だす［げんきを～］	cheer oneself up
広告	こうこく	advertisement
美容院	びよういん	beauty parlor
車いす	くるまいす	wheelchair
寄付する［病院に車いすを～］	きふする［びょういんにくるまいすを～］	donate [a wheelchair to the hospital]
グレー		grey
地味［な］	じみ［な］	plain, understated
原爆	げんばく	atomic bomb
ただ一つ	ただひとつ	only, unique
恐ろしさ	おそろしさ	horror
ダイナマイト		dynamite
自宅	じたく	one's home
あわてる		panic, get flustered
落ち着く	おちつく	calm down

11

行動する	こうどうする	act
のんびりする		spend one's time leisurely
シューズ		shoes
つながる		connect, get through [on the telephone]
［電話が～］	［でんわが～］	
遺跡	いせき	ruins, remains
発掘	はっくつ	excavation
これまでに		until now
南極	なんきょく	South Pole
探検	たんけん	exploration
世界遺産	せかいいさん	World Heritage (site)
価値	かち	worth, value
やっぱり		after all is said and done, at the end of the day (conversational form of やはり)
流氷	りゅうひょう	ice floe
自由行動	じゆうこうどう	acting at one's own discretion
提案する	ていあんする	propose, suggest
軽く	かるく	[do] light [exercise]
［～体操する］	［～たいそうする］	
乗り物	のりもの	vehicle, means of transport
酔う［乗り物に～］	よう［のりものに～］	feel [travel] sick
コメント		comment
さらに		furthermore
仮装	かそう	disguise, fancy dress
染める	そめる	dye
黄金	おうごん	gold
伝説	でんせつ	legend
いくつか		several
屋根	やね	roof
農作物	のうさくぶつ	crop
金銀	きんぎん	gold and silver
治める	おさめる	control

掌	てのひら	palm of the hand
後半	こうはん	latter part
くぎ		nail
村人	むらびと	villager
かける［費用を～］	［ひようを～］	spend [money]
向き	むき	(wind) direction
抵抗	ていこう	resistance
～層	～そう	layered
蚕	かいこ	silkworm
火薬	かやく	gunpowder
製造する	せいぞうする	manufacture
送る［生活を～］	おくる［せいかつを～］	lead [one's life]
家内産業	かないさんぎょう	cottage industry
年貢	ねんぐ	land tax, annual tribute
期待する	きたいする	expect, hope for
地	ち	land
前半	ぜんはん	first half
やってくる		come along, turn up
住み着く	すみつく	settle down, take up residence
一族	いちぞく	family
～城［帰雲～］	～じょう［かえりくも～］	～ castle [Kaerikumo ～]
城	しろ	castle
掘り当てる	ほりあてる	strike (gold, etc.)
権力者	けんりょくしゃ	powerful person
飢きん	ききん	famine
～軒	～けん	(counter for houses)
数百人	すうひゃくにん	several hundred people (cf. 数十人(すうじゅうにん)：several dozen people, 数千人(すうせんにん)：several thousand people)
一人残らず	ひとりのこらず	to the last man
消える	きえる	be wiped out

11

保管する	ほかんする	keep, store
兆	ちょう	trillion
分ける［いくつかに～］	わける	separate [into several parts]
積もる［雪が～］	つもる［ゆきが～］	[snow] accumulate
気候	きこう	climate
観光案内	かんこうあんない	tourist information
観光地	かんこうち	tourist spot

11

～っていうのはどうですか。　　How about....

When asked for advice, this expression indicates that you are merely making a suggestion, leaving it up to the person you are advising whether to adopt it or not.

それも悪（わる）くないですね。　　Yes, that's not bad either.

それもそうですね。　　Yes, I suppose that's right.

けど、……。　　But....

それも悪（わる）くないですけど……。　　That's not a bad idea, either, but....

Giving one's own opinion while acknowledging that the other person's opinion also has merit.

ノーベル	Alfred Bernhard Nobel : Swedish scientist who invented dynamite. 1833–1896.
モーツァルト	Wolfgang Amadeus Mozart : Austrian composer of over six hundred works including 'The Marriage of Figaro.' 1756–1791.
首里城（しゅりじょう）	Shuri Castle : Former castle of Ryukyu Kingdom, at Shuri, Okinawa.
雪祭り（ゆきまつり）	Snow Festival : Tourist festival held in Sapporo, Hokkaido, famous for its giant snow sculptures and illuminated trees.
白川郷（しらかわごう）	Shirakawa-go : Mountain village on upper reaches of River Sho in Gifu Prefecture, where extended families have traditionally lived together in large houses built in the gassho-zukuri style.

白神山地（しらかみさんち）	Shirakami Sanchi：Mountainous area on border of Aomori and Akita Prefectures, with Shirakamidake at its center. Contains one of the world's largest primeval Siebold's Beech forests.
厳島神社（いつくしまじんじゃ）	Itsukushima Shrine：Beautiful shrine in Miyajima, Hiroshima Prefecture, with buildings constructed in the sea. Rich in historic remains and national treasures.
屋久島（やくしま）	Yakushima：One of the Osumi Islands in Kagoshima Prefecture, covered with virgin forest of Japanese cedars (*Cryptomeria Japonica*) called Yakusugi, some said to be several thousand years old.
知床（しれとこ）	Shiretoko：A long, thin peninsula on the north-eastern tip of Hokkaido, which projects into the Sea of Okhotsk and whose coastline is cliffs.
原爆ドーム（げんばくドーム）	A-Bomb Dome：Hiroshima Peace Memorial (the remains of a building destroyed when the atomic bomb was dropped on Hiroshima on 6th August 1945).
合掌造り（がっしょうづくり）	Gassho-zukuri：Style of private dwellings in the Hida region, built for large families and sericulture, with steeply-pitched roofs to withstand heavy snowfalls.
江戸時代（えどじだい）	Edo Period：Same as Tokugawa Period, with Shogunate seated in Edo (present-day Tokyo). 1603–1867.
内ヶ嶋為氏（うちがしまためうじ）	Uchigashima Tameuji：Muromachi-period military commander who constructed Kaerikumo Castle in Shirakawa-go.
帰雲城（かえりくもじょう）	Kaerikumo Castle：Built by Uchigashima Tameuji at Shirakawa-go, Gifu Prefecture, in about 1464. Destroyed in 1586 by the Great Tensho Earthquake.
織田信長（おだのぶなが）	Oda Nobunaga：Military leader in the Azuchi-Momoyama period of the Sengoku (Warring States) period. 1534–1582.

Lesson 12

演奏会	えんそうかい	concert, recital
報告書	ほうこくしょ	report
あくび		yawn
犯人	はんにん	criminal
追いかける	おいかける	chase
作業	さぎょう	work
スープ		soup
こぼす		spill
シャッター		shutter
スプレー		spray
落書きする	らくがきする	draw graffiti, scribble
夜中	よなか	in the middle of the night
日	ひ	sunshine
当たる［日が～］	あたる［ひが～］	get [sunshine]
暮らす	くらす	live
書道	しょどう	calligraphy
蛍光灯	けいこうとう	fluorescent light
メニュー		menu
バイク		motorbike
目覚まし時計	めざましどけい	alarm clock
鳴る	なる	go off
温暖［な］	おんだん［な］	mild
家事	かじ	housework
ぐっすり［～眠る］	［～ねむる］	soundly [sleep]
迷惑	めいわく	nuisance, trouble
かける［迷惑を～］	［めいわくを～］	cause [trouble]
風邪薬	かぜぐすり	cold medicine
乗り遅れる	のりおくれる	miss (a bus, train, etc.)
苦情	くじょう	complaint

遅く	おそく	late
［お］帰り	［お］かえり	coming home
あまり		too
どうしても		inevitably, like it or not
自治会	じちかい	community association, residents' association
役員	やくいん	officer
ＤＶＤ	ディーブイディー	DVD
座談会	ざだんかい	round-table discussion
カルチャーショック		culture shock
受ける［ショックを～］	うける	get/receive [a shock]
それまで		until then, before
騒々しい	そうぞうしい	noisy
アナウンス		announcement
分かれる［意見が～］	わかれる［いけんが～］	be divided [opinion ～]
奥様	おくさま	housewife
おいでいただく		kindly come
苦労	くろう	hardship
中略	ちゅうりゃく	several paragraphs omitted
おかしな		funny
サンダル		sandal
ピーピー		whistling sound (of a kettle)
たまらない		cannot stand
都会	とかい	city
住宅地	じゅうたくち	residential area
虫	むし	insect
虫の音	むしのね	sound of insects
車内	しゃない	inside a vehicle
ホーム		platform
加える	くわえる	add

さっぱり[～ない]		[not] completely
乗客	じょうきゃく	passenger
安全性	あんぜんせい	safety
配慮する	はいりょする	consider
含む	ふくむ	include
チャイム		chime
発車ベル	はっしゃベル	train departure bell
必ずしも[～ない]	かならずしも	[not] necessarily
近所づきあい	きんじょづきあい	socializing with neighbors
コマーシャル		commercial

気(き)がつきませんでした。 — I didn't notice that.

どうしても…… — inevitably, always

Communicating that you feel something is impossible, after having given due consideration to the circumstances.

それはわかりますけど、…… — I understand that, but....

Indicating that you understand how the speaker feels, but it is nevertheless a problem for you.

どちらかと言(い)えば…… — On the whole....

いい勉強(べんきょう)になる — good for learning

ハンガリー	Hungary
ブダペスト	Budapest
バンコク	Bangkok
宇都宮(うつのみや)	Utsunomiya : Tochigi prefectural capital, located in the center of the prefecture.
浦安(うらやす)	Urayasu : Tokyo satellite city, located on Tokyo Bay in the northwest of Chiba Prefecture, and home of Tokyo Disney Resort.

Part 2

Grammatical Notes

Lesson 1

1. ～てもらえませんか・～ていただけませんか
～てもらえないでしょうか・～ていただけないでしょうか

Vて -form ＋ { もらえませんか／いただけませんか
**　　　　　　　　もらえないでしょうか／いただけないでしょうか**

「～てもらえませんか」and「～ていただけませんか」are used when politely asking someone to do something:

① ちょっとペンを貸してもらえませんか。

Could you lend me your pen for a moment, please?

② コピー機の使い方を教えていただけませんか。

Would you show me how to use the copier, please?

Ref: 「～ていただけませんか（polite request）」：

いい先生を紹介していただけませんか。　（☞『みんなの日本語初級Ⅱ』Lesson 26）

「～てもらえないでしょうか」and「～ていただけないでしょうか」sound even politer and softer than「～てもらえませんか」and「～ていただけませんか」：

③ すみません、子どもが寝ているので、もう少し静かにしてもらえないでしょうか。

Excuse me, my child's asleep, so would you mind being a little quieter, please?

④ 申し訳ございませんが、子どもを預っていただけないでしょうか。

I'm very sorry to trouble you, but could you possibly look after my child for me?

2. ～のようだ・～のような～・～のように…（simile; illustration）

Nの ＋ { ようだ
**　　　　ようなN**
**　　　　ようにV／いA／なA**

「～のようだ」is used at the end of a sentence when describing the characteristics of one noun (N_1) by likening it to another noun (N_2) (a simile):

① あの病院はホテルのようだ。　That hospital is like a hotel.

② このお酒はジュースのようだ。　This cocktail tastes like juice.

「～のようだ」is changed into「～のような」when modifying a noun:

③ 田中さんはホテルのような病院に入院している。

Mr. Tanaka is in a hospital like a hotel.

④ わたしはジュースのようなお酒しか飲まない。

I only drink cocktails that taste like juice.

「のようだ」is changed into「のように」when modifying a verb or an adjective:

⑤ 田中さんが入院している病院はホテルのようにきれいだ。

The hospital Mr. Tanaka is in is as nice as a hotel.

⑥ このお酒はジュースのように甘い。　This cocktail tastes as sweet as juice.

「～のような」is mostly used to describe something by citing N2 as an example (illustration):

⑦ 夫は、カレーのような簡単な料理しか作れません。

My husband can only cook simple dishes like curry.

⑧ 「アポ」のような外来語は、外国人にはとても難しい。

Loanwords like 'apo' are very difficult for non-Japanese people.

Ref: 「…ようだ（guessing from a situation）」:

人が大勢集まっていますね。

…事故のようですね。パトカーと救急車が来ていますよ。

(☞『みんなの日本語初級Ⅱ』Lesson 47)

3. ～ことは／が／を

V dic. -form ＋ こと ＋ は／が／を

Adding「～こと」turns a verb into a gerund;「こと」is used to nominalize the verb:

① 朝早く起きることは健康にいい。

Getting up early in the morning is good for the health.

② 田中さんは踊ることが好きです。　Mr. Tanaka likes dancing.

③ 優勝することを目指しています。　I'm aiming to win the championship.

Ref: 「V dic. -form ＋ ことができます／ことです」:

わたしはピアノを弾くことができます。

わたしの趣味は映画を見ることです。　(☞『みんなの日本語初級Ⅰ』Lesson 18)

1

4. ～を～と言(い)う

N_1 を N_2 と言(い)う

「～を～と言(い)う」is used when telling someone the name (N_2) of a thing or an event (N_1).

① 1月(いちがつ)1日(ついたち)を元日(がんじつ)と言(い)います。

We call the 1st of January 'Ganjitsu' (New Year's Day).

② 正月(しょうがつ)に神社(じんじゃ)やお寺(てら)に行(い)くことを初詣(はつもう)でと言(い)う。

We call visiting a shrine or temple at New Year 'Hatsumode.'

5. ～という～

N_1 という N_2

「～という～」is used to quote the name or title of a thing or person that the listener/reader may not know about. N_1 is a person's name or other proper noun, while N_2 is a common noun:

① 夏目漱石(なつめそうせき)という小説家(しょうせつか)を知(し)っていますか。

Have you heard of the novelist called Natsume Soseki?

② 昨日(きのう)、「スター・ウォーズ」という映画(えいが)を見(み)ました。

Yesterday I saw a film called 'Star Wars.'

6. いつ／どこ／何(なに)／だれ／どんなに～ても

V て -form
い A　ー~~い~~ → くて
な A ｝+ で
N ｝+ で
(all of the above) ＋ も

These express something that happens under all circumstances, whatever they might be. Use the form「ても」after「いつ」,「どこ」,「何(なに)」,「だれ」,「どんなに」, etc.:

① 世界中(せかいじゅう)どこにいても家族(かぞく)のことを忘(わす)れません。

Wherever I am in the world, I never forget my family.

② 何度(なんど)聞(き)いても同(おな)じことしか教(おし)えてくれない。

However many times I ask, they only tell me the same thing.

③ だれが何(なん)と言(い)っても考(かんが)えを変(か)えません。

I'm not going to change my opinion, no matter what anyone says.

④　どんなに高くても買いたいです。

I want to buy it, regardless of how expensive it might be.

With a noun, the expression takes the form「どんな N でも」,「どの N でも」or「どんなに～ N でも」:

⑤　どんな人でも優しい心を持っているはずだ。

I'm convinced that everyone, whoever he may be, is kind at heart.

⑥　正月になると、どの神社でも人がいっぱいだ。

When New Year arrives, shrines everywhere are packed with people.

⑦　どんなに丈夫なかばんでも長く使えば、壊れてしまうこともある。

However strong a suitcase might be, it can break if you use it for a long time.

Ref:「～ても（adversative conjunction）」: いくら考えても、わかりません。

（☞『みんなの日本語初級 I』Lesson 25）

話す・聞く

～じゃなくて、～

The expression「N1 じゃなくて、N2」negates N1 and proposes N2 instead:

①　これはペンじゃなくて、チョコレートです。食べられますよ。

This isn't a pen, it's chocolate. It's edible, you know.

②　京都ではお寺を見ましょうか。

…お寺じゃなくて、若い人が行くようなにぎやかなところに行きたいです。

Shall we go to see some temples while we're in Kyoto?

Not temples. I'd rather go somewhere lively, where young people go.

読む・書く

…のだ・…のではない

V / い A } **plain form**
な A / N } **plain form** **ーだ → な**
} **+** { **のだ** / **のではない**

「…のです」can be used in the following form when indicating a result that has arisen for a particular reason, or a guess based on certain logical grounds:

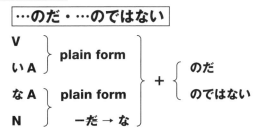

① 3時の飛行機に乗らなければなりません。それで、わたしは急いでいるのです。

I have to get on the 3 o'clock plane, so I'm in a hurry.

（reason ／ logical ground）（だから／それで）（result ／ guess）

② 彼は日本に留学します。それで日本語を勉強しているのです。

He's going to college in Japan. That's why he's learning Japanese.

「…のではない」is used to negate everything except the final part of the sentence.

For example, in ③, the 'all by myself' part is negated:

③ このレポートは一人で書いたのではありません。

I didn't write this report all by myself.

cf. ×このレポートは一人で書きませんでした。

何人も、何回も、何枚も…

「何 + counter（人、回、枚…）+ も」indicates a large number of something:

① マンションの前にパトカーが何台も止まっています。

There are a lot of police cars parked in front of the apartment block.

Lesson 2

1. (1) (2) ～たら、～た

Vたら、{V・A} た

(1)「Xたら、Yた」indicates that Y happened as a result of an action (X):

① 薬を飲んだら、元気になりました。

I felt better after I had taken the medicine.

② カーテンを変えたら、部屋が明るくなった。

The room became brighter after I changed the curtains.

(2) It can also indicate that Y was discovered as a result of an action (X):

③ 家に帰ったら、猫がいなかった。

After getting home, I noticed the cat wasn't there.

④ かばんを開けたら、財布がなくなっていた。

When I opened my bag, I found that my purse was missing.

⑤ 50年前の古いお酒を飲んでみたら、おいしかった。

On trying the fifty-year-old sake, I found it to be delicious.

The same meanings as in (1) and (2) can also be expressed by「Xと、Yた」:

⑥ 薬を飲むと、元気になりました。　I felt better after taking the medicine.

⑦ 家に帰ると、猫がいなかった。

When I got home, I found the cat wasn't there.

Ref: 「～たら (subjunctive)」: お金があったら、旅行します。

「～たら (perfective)」: 10時になったら、出かけましょう。

(☞『みんなの日本語初級 I』Lesson 25)

2. ～というのは～のことだ・～というのは…ということだ

Nというのは { Nの / S (plain form) という } + ことだ

「Xというのは～のことだ」and「Xというのは…ということだ」are expressions used when explaining the meaning of a term (X).

① 3Kというのは汚い、きつい、危険な仕事のことだ。

'3D' means dirty, difficult and dangerous work.

② PCというのはパソコンのことです。　'PC' stands for 'personal computer.'

③ 禁煙というのはたばこを吸ってはいけないということです。

'禁煙' means that smoking is prohibited.

④ 駐車違反というのは車を止めてはいけない場所に車を止めたということです。

'駐車違反' means that you have parked a car in a place where a car should not be parked.

2

3. …という～

S (plain form) ＋ という N (noun expressing an utterance or thought)

The form「…という～」is used when giving the details of a noun signifying an utterance or thought, such as「話、うわさ、考え、意見、意志、批判、ニュース」('talk,' rumor,' 'thought,' 'opinion,' 'intention,' 'criticism,' or 'news'):

① 昔ここは海だったという話を知っていますか。

Did you know that they say this area used to be under the sea?

② 田中さんがもうすぐ会社を辞めるといううわさを聞きました。

I heard a rumor that Mr. Tanaka is about to leave the company.

③ カリナさんは、研究室は禁煙にしたほうがいいという意見を持っている。

Karina is of the opinion that it would be better to ban smoking in the office.

4. …ように言う／注意する／伝える／頼む

V dic. -form
V ない -form　－ない } **ように ＋ V（言う、注意する、伝える、頼む）(say, warn, tell, ask)**

This is used when reporting the details of an instruction or request. When the instruction or request is in direct speech, the sentence takes the form「～なさい」,「～てはいけません」or「～てください」:

① 学生に図書館で物を食べないように注意しました。

I warned the students not to eat in the library.

→ 学生に「図書館で物を食べてはいけません」と注意しました。

I warned the students, saying, "You mustn't eat in the library."

② この仕事を今日中にやるように頼まれました。

I was asked to finish this job today.

→「この仕事を今日中にやってください」と頼まれました。

"Please finish this job today," I was asked.

③ 子どもたちに早く寝るように言いました。 I told the children to go to bed early.

→ 子どもたちに「早く寝なさい」と言いました。

I said to the children, "Go to bed early."

Note that ～なさい is an expression indicating an instruction or order. It is only used in certain situations, such as when parents talk to their children. It is also used for instructions on examination papers and so on.

5. ～みたいだ・～みたいな～・～みたいに…（simile / illustration）

N { **みたいだ** / **みたいな N** / **みたいに V／い A／な A** }

「～ようだ」and「～みたいだ」mean the same, but「～みたいだ」is less formal:

① わあ、このお酒、ジュースみたいだね。

Whoa! This cocktail tastes like juice, doesn't it!

② わたしはジュースみたいなお酒しか飲まない。

I only drink cocktails that resemble juice.

③ このお酒はジュースみたいに甘いよ。 Hey, this cocktail is as sweet as juice.

④ 夫は、カレーみたいな簡単な料理しか作れません。

My hubby can only cook easy stuff like curry.

Ref: 「～のようだ・～のような～・～のように…」:

あの病院はホテルのようだ。 （☞『みんなの日本語中級Ⅰ』Lesson 1）

話す・聞く

～ところ

「～ところ」means「～とき」(when), but it is only used in conjunction with certain words in polite situations, such as「お忙しいところ」(when you're busy),「お休みのところ」(when you're resting),「お急ぎのところ」(when you're in a hurry) and「お疲れのところ」(when you're tired). It is used when thanking someone or asking someone to do something:

① お忙しいところ、すみません。ちょっとお願いがあるんですが。

I'm sorry to bother you when you're so busy, but I have a little favor to ask....

② お休みのところ、手伝ってくださって、ありがとうございました。

Thank you very much for helping me during your time off.

Lesson 3

1. ～（さ）せてもらえませんか・～（さ）せていただけませんか
～（さ）せてもらえないでしょうか・～（さ）せていただけないでしょうか

V（さ）せて ＋ { もらえませんか／いただけませんか ／ もらえないでしょうか／いただけないでしょうか }

These expressions are used when asking someone for permission to do something:

① すみません。このパンフレットをコピーさせてもらえませんか。

Excuse me, may I copy this pamphlet?

② 月曜日の店長会議で報告させていただけませんか。

Could I make a report at the store manager's meeting on Monday?

③ 一度、工場を見学させていただけないでしょうか。

I wonder if we might be allowed to tour the factory sometime?

「～させていただけませんか」is politer than「～させてもらえませんか」, and「～させていただけないでしょうか」is politer than「～させていただけませんか」:

Ref: 「～させていただけませんか（polite request）」：しばらくここに車を止めさせていただけませんか。

（☞『みんなの日本語初級Ⅱ』Lesson 48）

2.（1） …ことにする

V dic. -form ／ Vない -form　－ない } ＋ ことにする

「Vする／Vしないことにする」is used to indicate a decision to do or not to do V:

① 来年結婚することにしました。　We've decided to get married next year.

② 今晩は外で食事をすることにしよう。　I have decided to eat out tonight.

2.（2） …ことにしている

V dic. -form ／ Vない -form　－ない } ＋ ことにしている

「Vする／Vしないことにしている」indicates a habit one previously decided to or not to continue to do:

① 毎週日曜日の夜は外で食事をすることにしている。

We make it a rule to eat out on Sunday evening.

② ダイエットしているので、お菓子を食べないことにしている。

I make it a rule not to eat any sweet things, because I'm on a diet.

3.（1） …ことになる

V dic. -form
V ない -form　－ない } **＋ ことになる**

「V することになる」and「V しないことになる」indicate a decision that something is to happen or not.「ことにする」is used to focus on who is going to take an action, while「ことになる」is used to focus on an action or event that happens voluntarily:

① 来月アメリカへ出張することになりました。

(It has been decided that) I'm to go on a business trip to the States next month.

② 中国へは田中さんが行くことになるでしょう。

It will probably be Mr. Tanaka who is chosen to go to China.

However, even when one has made the decision oneself,「ことになる」may be used in order to play down the fact that it was one's own decision:

③ 部長、実は、今年の秋に結婚することになりました。結婚式に出席していただけないでしょうか。

Department Manager, I'm getting married this autumn, and I was wondering if you would be kind enough to come to the wedding.

3.（2） …ことになっている

V dic. -form
V ない -form　－ない } **＋ ことになっている**

When in the form「V する／V しないことになっている」, these expressions indicate that something has been scheduled, or established as a rule:

① あしたの朝 9 時から試験を行うことになっています。

A test is scheduled for 9:00 a.m. tomorrow.

② うちでは夜 9 時以降はテレビをつけないことになっている。

In our house, the television is not switched on after 9:00 p.m.

4. ～てほしい・～ないでほしい

Vて-form } + **ほしい**
Vない-form −ないで }

(1)「NにVてほしい」is used to indicate wishing that someone else (N) would do something (V):

① わたしは息子に優しい人になってほしいです。

I would like my son to become a kind person.

「Nに」can be omitted when N is known:

② このごろ自転車を利用する人が多いが、規則を守って乗ってほしい。

Many people use bicycles these days, but I wish they would obey the regulations when they ride.

Wishing that N would not do V is shown by the negative form,「Vないでほしい」:

③ こんなところにごみを捨てないでほしい。

I wish people wouldn't dump rubbish in places like this.

Although they become expressions of request or instruction when used about someone else's actions, they would be too direct if used without any modification, so they are often softened by appending expressions like「のですが／んですが」:

④ すみません、ちょっと手伝ってほしいんですが。

Excuse me, but I'd like you to help me for a moment if you could.

(2) They can also be used about matters other than people's actions, in which case,「Nが」is used instead of「Nに」:

⑤ 早く春が来てほしい。 I wish spring would hurry up and come.

⑥ あしたは雨が降らないでほしい。 I hope it doesn't rain tomorrow.

5. (1) ～そうな～・～そうに…

Vます-form
いA −~~い~~ } + { **そうなN** / **そうにV** }
なA

「Vます−そうだ」has a different meaning when appended to a verb（「V−plain−そうだ」）than when appended to an adjective（「Aそうだ」）.「Vそうだ」indicates that the speaker predicts that there is a high probability of V occurring, or indicates signs that V will occur:

① ミラーさん、シャツのボタンが取れそうですよ。

Mr. Miller, one of your shirt buttons looks like it's about to come off.

② 雨が降りそうなときは、洗濯しません。

When it looks like rain, I don't do any washing.

「Aそうだ」means that something appears to be A:

③ ワンさんの隣にいる学生はまじめそうですね。

The student next to Mr. Wong appears serious-minded, doesn't he?

④ このケーキはおいしそうですね。　This cake looks yummy, doesn't it?

⑤ 子どもたちが楽しそうに遊んでいます。

The children seem to be playing happily.

When「Vそうだ」(expressing a prediction, or an indication of a future event) and「Aそうだ」(indicating an external appearance) modify a noun, they take the form「そうなN」. When they modify a verb, they take the form「そうにV」:

⑥ 雨が降りそうなときは、洗濯しません。

I don't do any washing when it looks like rain.

⑦ おいしそうなケーキがありますね。　There's a yummy-looking cake, isn't there?

⑧ 子どもたちが楽しそうに遊んでいます。

The children seem to be playing happily.

Ref: 「～そうだ（prediction, appearance）」:

今にも雨が降りそうです。

この料理は辛そうです。

ミラーさんはうれしそうです。　（☞『みんなの日本語初級Ⅱ』Lesson 43）

5.（2） ～なさそう

いA　－~~い~~ → く

なA / N　－~~だ~~ → では（じゃ）

＋ なさそう

The negative form of「Aそうだ」is not「～ないそうだ」but「～なさそうだ」. It means that the article in question does not appear to be A or is not thought to be A:

① あの映画はあまりおもしろくなさそうですね。

That film doesn't look very interesting, does it?

② この機械はそんなに複雑じゃ（では）なさそうです。

This machine doesn't look that complicated.

③ 彼は学生ではなさそうです。　He doesn't look like a student.

5.（3） ～そうもない

V ます -form　＋ そうもない

The negative form of「V ます－そうだ」is「V ます－そうもない」and indicates the prediction that V will probably not occur:

① 今日は仕事がたくさんあるので、5時に帰れそうもありません。

I've got a lot of work to do today, so it doesn't look as if I'll be able to leave at five.

② この雨はまだやみそうもないですね。

This rain doesn't look like stopping yet, does it?

話す・聞く

～たあと、…

V たあと、…

「V たあと、…」indicates the following on of a situation or circumstance（…）from V:

① じゃ、来週の月曜日会議が終わった｛あと／あとで｝、お会いしましょうか。

OK, shall we get together after the meeting has finished next Monday?

When「…」contains words like「いる」or「ある」,「あとで」sounds awkward:

② 日曜日は朝食を食べた｛○あと／×あとで｝、どこへも行かず家でテレビを見ていました。

We didn't go anywhere after having breakfast on Sunday; we stayed at home and watched TV.

③ 授業が終わった｛○あと／×あとで｝、学生が2、3人まだ教室に残っていました。

After the lesson was over, two or three students were still in the classroom, staying behind.

Lesson 4

1. …ということだ（reported speech）

S（plain form）＋ ということだ

(1)「Xということだ」is a reported-speech expression similar to「Xそうだ」and is used when reporting what someone else has said (X), or what people in general say:

① 山田さんから電話があったのですが、約束の時間に少し遅れるということです。

Mr. Yamada phoned; he said he would be a little late for the appointment.

② 近くにいた人の話によると、トラックから急に荷物が落ちたということです。

According to the bystanders, the load suddenly fell off the truck.

It can also take the form「とのことです」, but this tends to be more like written language:

③ （手紙文）先日、ワンさんに会いました。ワンさんから先生によろしくとのことです。

(From a letter) I saw Mr. Wong the other day. He asked me to give you his regards.

(2)「Xということですね」can be used when repeating what someone has just said, in order to confirm it:

④ A：部長に30分ほど遅れると伝えてください。

Please tell the Department Manager that I'll be about thirty minutes late.

B：はい、わかりました。30分ほど遅れるということですね。

Yes, I understand. You'll be about thirty minutes late, right?

2. …の・…の？

S（plain form）＋ { の / の？ }

This is an informal form of「…のですか」, used when conversing with someone you are on familiar terms with:

① どこへ行くの？　Where are you off to?

…ちょっと郵便局へ。　I'm just popping down to the post office.

② 元気(げんき)がないね。先生(せんせい)にしかられたの？

You look a bit down in the dumps. Did your teacher tell you off ?

…うん。　Yeah.

③ どうしたの？　What's up?

…お母(かあ)さんがいないの。　Mum's not here.

Ref: 「…のです／んです」is an expression used for emphasizing a cause, reason, logical basis or other explanation. While「…んです」is conversational,「…のです」is used in writing.

(☞『みんなの日本語初級Ⅱ』Lesson 26)

3. ～ちゃう・～とく・～てる

〈How to create forms〉

Vてしまう　→　Vちゃう

Vておく　→　Vとく

Vている　→　Vてる

(1)「～てしまう」becomes「～ちゃう」in spoken language:

① 行(い)ってしまいます → 行(い)っちゃいます

② 読(よ)んでしまった → 読(よ)んじゃった

③ 見(み)てしまった → 見(み)ちゃった

(2)「～ておく」becomes「～とく」in spoken language:

④ 見(み)ておきます → 見(み)ときます

⑤ 作(つく)っておこう → 作(つく)っとこう

⑥ 読(よ)んでおいてください → 読(よ)んどいてください

(3)「～ている」becomes「～てる」in spoken language:

⑦ 走(はし)っている → 走(はし)ってる

⑧ 読(よ)んでいる → 読(よ)んでる

⑨ 見(み)ていない → 見(み)てない

4. ～（さ）せられる・～される（causative-passive）

〈How to create forms〉

VⅠ：ない-form　＋せられる／される

VⅡ：ない-form　＋させられる

VⅢ：する → させられる

＊来(く)る → 来(こ)させられる

(1) This expression combines the causative and passive:

① 太郎君は掃除をしました。Taro cleaned up.

→ 先生は太郎君に掃除をさせました。

(causative) The teacher made Taro clean up.

→ 太郎君は先生に掃除をさせられました。

(causative-passive) Taro was made to clean up by the teacher.

(2) The sentence pattern「N_1 は N_2 に V させられる」is the basic causative-passive form, but sometimes「N_2 に」is not specified. However, in either case, it means that N_1 does V not through their own volition, but because they were made to do so by someone else:

② 昨日の忘年会ではカラオケを {歌わせられた／歌わされた}。

I was made to sing a karaoke song at yesterday's year-end party.

③ この会議では毎月新しい問題について研究したことを発表させられます。

At this conference, we are made to present what we have found out about a new issue every month.

5. ～である（である style）

N
なA } **＋ である**

～ている ＋ のである

「～である」means the same as「～だ」but is more formal. It is often used in writing, particularly for dissertations and the like:

① 失敗は成功の母である。 Failure is the stepping-stone to success.

② このような事件を起こしたことは非常に残念である。

To have brought about an affair like this is extremely regrettable.

③ ここは去年まで山であった。

This area was mountainous forest until last year.

In the「である」style,「～のだ」becomes「～のである」:

④ 世界中の人々が地球の平和を願っているのである。

People all over the world are hoping for world peace.

6. ～ま~~す~~、～ま~~す~~、…・～く~~て~~、～く~~て~~、…（suspended form）

〈How to create forms〉

V　：Vます-form　－~~ます~~（います → おり）

いA：いA　－~~い~~ → く

なA：なA　－で

N　：N　　－で

(1) The suspended form of the verb (the same form as the ます-form) is used in the form「V$_1$（ます-form）、V$_2$」and marks a succession or concurrency of events, in the same way as「V$_1$（て-form）、V$_2$」:

① 朝起きたら、まず顔を洗い、コーヒーを飲み、新聞を読みます。

After I get up in the morning, I first wash my face, then drink coffee and read the paper.

② 彼とは学生時代、よく遊び、よく話し、よく飲んだ。

I often fooled around, talked and went drinking with him when we were at university.

(2) The suspended form of「いる」is「おり」:

③ 兄は東京におり、姉は大阪にいます。

My elder brother is in Tokyo and my elder sister in Osaka.

(3) The suspended form of an adjective or noun indicates the coexistence of the meanings shown by each of the words:

④ マリアさんは、優しく、頭がよく、すばらしい女性だ。

Maria is a kind, intelligent, wonderful woman.

7. (1) ～（た）がる

Vます-form　＋ たがる

いA　－~~い~~ ｝＋ がる
なA

When attached, in the form「Nが～（た）がる」, to an adjective expressing emotion, this indicates that N's (someone else's) emotion is revealing itself in their expression or behavior. When N appears to want something (「～たい」), it takes the form「～たがる」:

① 太郎君は友達のおもちゃを欲しがる。　Taro covets his friends' toys.

② このチームが負けると、息子はすごく悔しがる。

My son will feel gutted if this team loses.

③ このごろの若者(わかもの)は、難(むずか)しい本(ほん)を読(よ)みたがらない。

Young people these days are disinclined to read difficult books.

7.（2）～（た）がっている

Vます-form ＋たがっている

いA　ー~~い~~ ｝ **＋がっている**
なA ｝

「～（た）がる」indicates a person's tendency to habitually behave in a way that demonstrates a particular emotion, aspiration, etc. When the person is behaving in that way at the present moment, the form「～（た）がっている」is used:

① 太郎君(たろうくん)は友達(ともだち)のおもちゃを欲(ほ)しがっている。

Taro has got his eye on his friend's toys.

② 好(す)きなチームが負(ま)けて、息子(むすこ)はすごく悔(くや)しがっている。

The team he likes has lost, and my son is feeling gutted.

8. …こと・…ということ

S（plain form）＋［という］こと＋case particle

なA ＋なこと／であること

（1）When a particle or other part of speech is appended to a sentence, the form「…こと＋particle」is used to nominalize the sentence（make it function as a noun）. The sentence that comes before「…こと」takes the plain form:

① 田中(たなか)さんが結婚(けっこん)したことを知(し)っていますか。

Did you know that Mr. Tanaka has got married?

② これは田中(たなか)さんの辞書(じしょ)ではないことがわかりました。

I realized that this is not Mr. Tanaka's dictionary.

When the sentence ends with a な A, the form「なA＋なこと」or「なA＋であること」is used:

③ 世界中(せかいじゅう)でこの漫画(まんが)が有名(ゆうめい)｛な／である｝ことを知(し)っていますか。

Did you know that this manga is world-famous?

（2）When the sentence is long and complicated,「という」must be used in front of「こと」in order to nominalize the sentence. In this case,「～ということ」is appended to the plain-form sentence:

④ 二十歳(はたち)になればだれでも結婚(けっこん)できるということを知(し)っていますか？

Did you know that anyone can get married once they turn twenty?

⑤ 日本(にほん)に来(き)てから、家族(かぞく)はとても大切(たいせつ)｛だ／である｝ということに初(はじ)めて気(き)がついた。

It was only after coming to Japan that I realized how important my family is.

⑥ この辺(あた)りは昔(むかし)、海(うみ)｛だった／であった｝ということは、あまり知(し)られていない。

It is not very well known that the area round here used to be under the sea.

Ref: 「こと」：朝早(あさはや)く起(お)きることは健康(けんこう)にいい。 （☞『みんなの日本語中級Ｉ』Lesson 1）

東京(とうきょう)へ行(い)っても、大阪(おおさか)のことを忘(わす)れないでくださいね。

（☞『みんなの日本語初級Ｉ』Lesson 25）

話(はな)す・聞(き)く

～の～（apposition）

「～の～」shows that N_1 and N_2 are identical. N_1 is a noun that shows an attribute of N_2, giving more information about it. It can also be expressed in the form「N_1である N_2」:

① 部長(ぶちょう)の田中(たなか)をご紹介(しょうかい)します。

I would like to introduce Mr. Tanaka, our Department Manager.

② あさっての金曜日(きんようび)はご都合(つごう)いかがですか。

Are you free the day after tomorrow, Friday?

～ましたら、…・～まして、…

V（polite form）＋｛たら・て｝、…

「たら」and the て-form can also be polite forms:

① 会議(かいぎ)が終(お)わりましたら、こちらからお電話(でんわ)させていただきます。

I will take the liberty of telephoning you when the meeting has finished.

② 本日(ほんじつ)は遠(とお)くから来(き)てくださいまして、ありがとうございました。

Thank you very much for travelling so far to be here today.

Lesson 5

1.（1） あ～・そ～（contextual demonstrative pronoun（conversational））

Demonstratives such as「あ～」and「そ～」can be used to refer to something that has cropped up in a conversation or appears in a text, as well as something that is physically present. In conversation, something directly known to both the speaker and the listener is indicated by「あ（あれ、あの、あそこ…）」. Something known to the speaker but not to the listener, or vice versa, is indicated by「そ（それ、その、そこ）」:

① さっき、山本さんに会ったよ。　I met Mr. Yamamoto just now.

…え、あの人、今日本にいるんですか。　Oh? Is he in Japan now?

② さっき、図書館でマリアさんという人に会ったんだけどね。その人、この学校で日本語を勉強したんだって。

I met someone called Maria in the library just now. She said she had studied Japanese at this school.

…そうですか。その人は何歳ぐらいですか。　Really? How old is she?

1.（2） そ～（contextual demonstrative pronoun（sentence））

In sentences,「そ（それ、その、そこ…）」is used to refer to something that appeared in the previous sentence:

① 会社を出たあと、駅のレストランで夕食を食べました。そのとき、財布を落としたんだと思います。

After leaving the office, I had dinner in the station restaurant. I think I dropped my wallet then.

② イギリスの人気小説が日本語に翻訳されました。それが今年日本でベストセラーになりました。

A popular British novel was translated into Japanese. Now it's become a best-seller in Japan this year.

2. …んじゃない？

V いA	plain form	+ [んじゃないですか]／んじゃない？
なA N	plain form −だ → な	

「…んじゃないですか」is an informal form of「…のではありませんか」. It is used in informal conversation when saying what the speaker is thinking:

① 元気がないですね。何か困っていることがあるんじゃないですか。

You look a bit glum. Is something bothering you, I wonder?

…ええ、実は……。 Yes, as a matter of fact....

「んじゃないですか」is sometimes shortened to「んじゃない」when used with someone with whom the speaker is on familiar terms. In formal conversation, it lengthens to「のではないでしょうか」:

② タワポンさん、少し太ったんじゃない。

Thawaphon, you've put on a little weight, haven't you?

…わかりますか。 Does it show?

3. ～たところに／で

V（motion verb）た -form ＋ ところ

Verbs indicating motion, such as「行く、渡る、曲がる、出る」(go, cross, turn, and emerge) are used in the form「V た -form ＋ところ」to indicate the position arrived at after the motion has taken place:

① あの信号を左へ曲がったところに、郵便局があります。

There's a post office just after you turn left at those traffic lights.

② 改札を出て、階段を上ったところで、待っていてください。

Go through the ticket barrier and wait at the top of the steps, please.

4.（1）（2） ～（よ）う（volitional form）とする／しない

V（よ）う ＋ とする／しない

(1)「V（よ）う (volitional form) とする／しない」indicates a situation that arises just before doing V, so「V する」does not actually take place. When applied in this way, it is usually used together with「～とき」,「～たら」, etc.:

① 家を出ようとしたとき、電話がかかってきた。

The phone rang as I was about to leave the house.

② 雨がやんだので、桜を撮ろうとしたら、カメラの電池が切れてしまった。

When I went to photograph the cherry blossoms because the rain had stopped, I found that my camera battery was flat.

(2) It can also indicate that someone is trying to do V:

③ 父は健康のためにたばこをやめようとしています。

My father is trying to give up smoking for the sake of his health.

④ あの日のことは、忘れようとしても忘れることができません。

I cannot forget what happened that day, even though I try.

(3)「V（volitional form）としない」indicates that a person does not intend to do V. It is usually used in reference to people other than oneself.

⑤ 妻は紅茶が好きで、お茶やコーヒーを飲もうとしない。

My wife likes black tea, and she has no interest in drinking green tea, coffee or anything like that.

⑥ 人の話を聞こうとしない人は、いつまでたっても自分の考えを変えることができません。

People who are not interested in listening to what others say can never change their opinion.

5. …のだろうか

V / **いA**	**plain form**	**+ のだろうか**
なA / **N**	**plain form** **ーだ → な**	

The expression「X のだろうか」is used when asking oneself whether X is true or not. It can also be used with an interrogative such as「どう」,「何」, or「いつ」to ask oneself a question:

① この店ではクレジットカードが使えるのだろうか。

I wonder if this shop takes credit cards.

② 大学院に入るためには、どうすればいいのだろうか。

I wonder what I need to do to get into postgraduate school.

It can also be used when asking someone else a question. Compared with「Xのですか」, which is more direct,「Xのでしょうか」is a gentler way of asking that does not demand an answer:

③ すみません。この店ではクレジットカードが使えるのでしょうか。

Excuse me, does this shop take credit cards.

It can also be used in the form「Xのだろうか」, without an interrogative, when one wants to suggest that X is not true, or that one does not think X:

④ このクラスでは日本語で話すチャンスがとても少ない。こんな勉強で会話が上手になるのだろうか。

There is very little opportunity to speak Japanese in this class. I wonder whether it is really possible to improve one's conversation skills with a study method like this?

6. ～との／での／からの／までの／への～

N + {case particle + の} + N

When a word with a case particle such as「と、で、から、まで、or へ」attached is used to modify a noun,「の」is appended to the particle, except if the particle is「に」, in which case「に」is changed to「へ」and「への」is used:

① 友達との北海道旅行は、とても楽しかったです。

The trip to Hokkaido with my friends was very enjoyable.

② 日本での研究はいかがでしたか。 How did your research in Japan go?

③ 国の両親からの手紙を読んで、泣いてしまった。

I was moved to tears when I read the letter from my parents back in my home country.

④ 先生へのお土産は何がいいでしょうか。

I wonder what would make a good souvenir for our teacher?

「の」is not appended to「が」or「を」either:

⑤ 田中さんの欠席を部長に伝えてください。

Please report Mr. Tanaka's absence to the Department Manager.

⑥ 大学院で医学の研究をするつもりです。

I intend to do medical research at postgraduate school.

7. …だろう・…だろうと思う（conjecture）

V / いA	plain form	+ だろう
なA / N	plain form —だ	+ だろう

(1)「…だろう」is the plain form of「…でしょう」and is used in sentences in the plain style. It is used to express one's opinion conjecturally rather than definitely:

① アジアの経済はこれからますます発展するだろう。

The Asian economy will probably develop more and more from now on.

② マリアさんの話を聞いて、ご両親もきっとびっくりされただろう。

I expect Maria's parents also got a shock when they heard what she had to say.

(2) In conversation, it is usual to append「と思う」and use it in the form「…だろうと思う」:

③ 鈴木君はいい教師になるだろうと思います。

I think that young Suzuki will probably become a good teacher.

④ この実験にはあと2、3週間はかかるだろうと思います。

I think that this experiment will probably take another two or three weeks.

Ref: 「～でしょう？（asking for confirmation）」:

7月に京都でお祭りがあるでしょう？ (☞『みんなの日本語初級Ⅰ』Lesson 21)

「～でしょう（conjecture）」: あしたは雪が降るでしょう。

(☞『みんなの日本語初級Ⅱ』Lesson 32)

話す・聞く

…から、～てください

V (polite form) + から、V てください

When used in this context,「…から」does not indicate a reason. It indicates some information that is a prerequisite for the request or instruction that follows:

① お金を入れるとボタンに電気がつきますから、それを押してください。

When you put some money in, the button lights up; then press that, please.

② 10分ぐらいで戻ってきますから、ここで待っていてくれますか。

I'll be back in about ten minutes; could you wait here, please?

読(よ)む・書(か)く

が／の

The「が」of the subject of a clause describing a noun can be replaced by「の」:

① 留学生(りゅうがくせい)｛が／の｝かいた絵(え)を見(み)ました。

I saw the pictures that the foreign students had painted.

② 田中(たなか)さん｛が／の｝作(つく)ったケーキはとてもおいしかった。

The cake that Mr. Tanaka made was scrumptious.

Lesson 6

1.（1）…て…・…って…（quoting）

S（plain form）＋ て／って…

The「と」used for quoting can become「て」or「って」in spoken language:

① 田中さんは昨日何て言っていましたか。 ←「と」

What did Mr. Tanaka say yesterday?

…今日は休むって言っていました。 ←「と」

He said that he was going to take today off.

② 店の前に「本日休業」って書いてありました。 ←「と」

There was a sign in front of the shop saying, 'Closed Today.'

6

The「という」in「〜という名前を持つ人／もの／ところ」can also become「って」:

③ 昨日、田山って人が来ましたよ。 ←「という」

Someone called Tayama came by yesterday.

1.（2）〜って…（topic）

S（plain form）
N plain form ーだ } **＋ って…**

「Xって」is used when asking about something (X) that the speaker does not know much about, or when the speaker is describing the nature or characteristics of X:

① ねえ、函館って、どんな町？ Say, what kind of city is Hakodate?

② メンタルトレーニングっておもしろい！ This 'mental training' is fun!

2.（1）〜つもりはない（negative intention）

V dic. -form ＋ つもりはない

(1)「〜つもりはない」is the negative form of「〜つもりだ」and means 'has no intention of':

① 卒業後は就職するつもりです。大学院に行くつもりはありません。

After I graduate, I plan to get a job. I don't intend to go to postgraduate school.

② 仕事が忙しいので、今夜のパーティーに出るつもりはない。

I'm busy with work today, so I'm not thinking of going to the party tonight.

「Vつもりはない」can be changed to「そのつもりはない」if the details of what V indicates are known:

③ A：1週間くらい休みを取ったらどうですか。

How about taking a week or so off?

B：いえ、そのつもりはありません。　No, I'm not going to do that.

(2) There are two negative forms of「～つもりだ」:「～つもりはない」and「～ないつもりだ」.「～つもりはない」is a stronger negative, and is used when strenuously denying what the other party has said, for example:

④ 新しいコンピューターが発売されました。いかがですか。

A new type of computer has been brought out. How about buying one?

…コンピューターは持っているから {○買うつもりはない／×買わないつもりだよ。}

I've already got a computer, so I have absolutely no intention of buying another one.

2. (2) ～つもりだった (past volition)

V dic. -form
Vない-form　ーない　} ＋ **つもりだった**

(1)「～つもりだった」is the past form of「～つもりだ」and means 'intended to':

① 電話するつもりでしたが、忘れてしまいました。すみません。

I meant to phone you, but I went and forgot. I'm sorry.

(2) It is often followed by words expressing a change of mind:

② パーティーには行かないつもりでしたが、おもしろそうなので行くことにしました。

I hadn't intended to go to the party, but it looked like it would be fun, so I decided to go after all.

Ref: 「～つもりだ (volition)」: 国へ帰っても、柔道を続けるつもりです。

(☞『みんなの日本語初級II』Lesson 31)

2.（3）～たつもり・～ているつもり

Vた -form
Vている
いA　　　　　**＋ つもり**
なA　ーな
Nの

「Xたつもり／Xているつもり」indicates that the agent thinks something is X. However, in reality, it may not be X at all, or it may be unknown whether it is X or not:

① 外国語を練習するときは、小さな子どもになったつもりで、大きな声を出してみるといい。

When practicing a foreign language, it is best to try speaking in a loud voice, as if one were a little child.

② かぎがかかっていませんでしたよ。 It was unlocked, you know.

…すみません、かけたつもりでした。 Sorry. I thought I'd locked it.

③ わたしは一生懸命やっているつもりです。 I think I'm trying really hard.

④ 若いつもりで無理をしたら、けがをしてしまった。

I went and injured myself, overdoing it as if I were young again.

⑤ 本当の研究発表のつもりで、みんなの前で話してください。

Please stand in front of the group and tell everyone, as if it were a real research presentation.

Ref: 「V dic. -form つもりです（intention to act）」:

国へ帰っても、柔道を続けるつもりです。 （☞『みんなの日本語初級Ⅱ』Lesson 31）

3. ～てばかりいる・～ばかり～ている

（1）Vて -form ＋ ばかりいる

（2）Nばかり ＋ V_t ている

（1）This indicates that an action is performed habitually or repeatedly, and that the speaker is critical of or dissatisfied with this:

① この猫は一日中、寝てばかりいる。 This cat just sleeps all day long.

② 弟はいつもコンピューターゲームをしてばかりいる。

My younger brother is always playing computer games.

(2) With a transitive verb,「ばかり」can come immediately after what it refers to:

③ 弟はいつもコンピューターゲームばかりしている。

Almost all my younger brother does is play computer games.

4. …とか…

N
S（plain form） } **+ とか**

(1)「…とか…とか」is used when enumerating several similar examples:

① 最近忙しくて、テレビのドラマとか映画とか見る時間がありません。

② 健康のためにテニスとか水泳とかを始めてみるといいですよ。

（☞『みんなの日本語初級Ⅱ』Lesson 36）

(2)「…」can be replaced by whole sentences:

③ 子どものとき、母に「勉強しろ」とか「たくさん食べなさい」とかよく言われました。

When I was a child, I was often told by my mother to "Go and study," "Eat up," and so on.

④ 今日のテストは「難しい」とか「問題が多すぎる」とか思った学生が多いようです。

It seems that a lot of students thought that today's test was "difficult," "contained too many questions," and so forth.

⑤ やせたいんです。どうしたらいいですか。

I want to lose weight. How should I go about it?

…毎日水泳をするとか、ジョギングをするとかすればいいですよ。

You should do something like swimming or jogging every day.

5. ～てくる（advent of a condition）

Vて-form + くる

「～てくる」indicates that a new event has happened, and that consequently something has become perceptible:

① 暗くなって、星が見えてきた。　It grew dark, and the stars came out.

② 隣の家からいいにおいがしてきた。

A good smell came wafting from the house next door.

6. ～てくる（approach）・～ていく（withdraw）

Vて-form ＋ { くる / いく

「～てくる」and「～ていく」are appended to motion verbs to show the direction of motion.「～てくる」indicates that the motion is towards the speaker, and「～ていく」indicates that the motion is away from the speaker:

① 兄(あに)が旅行(りょこう)から帰(かえ)ってきた。　My elder brother came back from his trip.

② 授業(じゅぎょう)のあと、学生(がくせい)たちはうちへ帰(かえ)っていった。

After the lesson, the students went home.

読(よ)む・書(か)く

こ～（contextual demonstrative pronoun）

「こ」in a sentence can indicate something that appears later in the sentence:

① 新聞(しんぶん)にこんなことが書(か)いてあった。最近(さいきん)の日本人(にほんじん)は家族(かぞく)みんなで休日(きゅうじつ)にコンピューターゲームを楽(たの)しむそうだ。

This was written in the newspaper: "Apparently, Japanese families these days enjoy playing computer games together on their days off."

Ref: 「あ～・そ～（contextual demonstrative pronoun（conversational））」
「そ～（contextual demonstrative pronoun（sentence））」
（☞『みんなの日本語中級Ⅰ』Lesson 5）

6

Lesson 7

1. (1) ～なくてはならない／いけない・～なくてもかまわない

V ない -form		+	**なくてはならない／いけない**
いA	**－~~い~~ → く**		**なくてもかまわない**
なA	**で**		
N	**で**		

(1)「～なくてはならない／いけない」indicates that「～」is obligatory or definitely necessary. It is the same as「～なければならない」:

① この薬は一日２回飲まなくてはならない。

This medicine must be taken twice a day.

② レポートは日本語でなくてはなりません。　The report has to be in Japanese.

(2)「～なくてもかまわない」indicates that「～」is not necessary. It is a politer expression than「～なくてもいいです」:

③ 熱が下がったら、薬を飲まなくてもかまわない。

Once your temperature has gone down, it's all right not to take the medicine.

④ 作文は長くなくてもかまいません。　The composition does not have to be very long.

Ref:「～なければならない (must be done regardless of whether the performer of the action wants to or not)」: 薬を飲まなければなりません。

「～なくてもいい (no need to perform the action)」: あした来なくてもいいです。

(☞『みんなの日本語初級 I』Lesson 17)

7

1. (2) ～なくちゃ／～なきゃ［いけない］

〈How to create forms〉

V なくてはいけない → V なくちゃ［いけない］

V なければいけない → V なきゃ［いけない］

In informal conversation,「なくてはいけない」can become「なくちゃいけない」and「なければいけない」can become「なきゃいけない」.「いけない」may be omitted.

2. …だけだ・［ただ］…だけでいい

（1）N ＋ だけ

（2）
V / いA — plain form
なA — plain form －だ → な
＋ だけだ / だけでいい

(1)「～だけ」is attached to a noun to indicate a limit. (☞『みんなの日本語初級 I』Lesson 11)

① 外国人の社員は一人だけいます。

② 休みは日曜日だけです。

(2) A verb or an adjective can precede「…だけ」, creating a predicate:

③ 何をしているの？…ただ、本を読んでいるだけです。

What are you doing?　I'm just reading a book.

④ 病気ですか？…ちょっと気分が悪いだけです。

Are you ill?　No, I'm just feeling a little poorly.

(3)「…するだけでいい」indicates that it is only necessary to perform the specified action (「…すること」) and nothing else:

⑤ 申し込みはどうするんですか？…　この紙に名前を書くだけでいいんです。

How do I apply?　All you have to do is to write your name on this piece of paper.

3. …かな (sentence-final particle)

V / いA — plain form
なA / N — plain form －だ
＋ かな

(1)「…かな」is used when posing a question that does not demand an answer:

① A：お父さんの誕生日のプレゼントは何がいいかな。

I wonder what I should get Dad for his birthday?

B：セーターはどうかな。　How about a pullover, I wonder?

(2) Using「…ないかな」for an invitation or request has a softening effect, making the invitation or request less direct:

② A：明日みんなで桜を見に行くんですが、先生もいっしょにいらっしゃらないかなと思いまして。

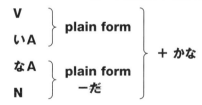

We're all going to see the cherry blossoms tomorrow, and I wondered whether you might not like to come with us.

B：桜ですか。いいですね。　The cherry blossoms, eh? That would be nice.

③ A：3時までにこの資料を全部コピーしなければならないんだけど、手伝ってくれないかな。

I have to get all of these materials copied by three o'clock, and I wondered whether you might not be able to help me.

B：いいよ。　No problem.

4.（1）～なんか…

N ＋ なんか

「～なんか」indicates that the speaker disparages「～」, attaching little importance to it. It is like「など」but is used in conversation:

① わたしの絵なんかみんなに見せないでください。絵が下手なんです。

Please don't go showing my pictures to everyone. I'm no good at painting.

4.（2）…なんて…

V
いA　} **plain form**　} **＋ なんて**
なA
N

（1）「X なんて Y」also indicates that the speaker disparages X and attaches little importance to it. It too is like「など」but is used in conversation:

① わたしの絵なんてみんなに見せないでください。絵が下手なんです。

Please don't go showing my pictures to everyone. I'm no good at painting.

（2）「X なんて」is also used to express criticism of X or display surprise concerning it. It is used in conversation:

② 昨日、大江さんという人から電話があったよ。

You had a phone call from someone called Oe yesterday.

…大江なんて（人）知りませんよ、わたし。

But I don't know anyone called Oe!

③ 先生が3年も前に事故にあって亡くなったなんて、知りませんでした。

I had no idea that our teacher had been killed in an accident and has been dead for three years!

④ 試験に一度で合格できたなんて、びっくりしました。

I was amazed when I passed the test at my first attempt!

⑤ ミラーさんがあんなに歌がうまいなんて、知りませんでした。

I had no idea that Mr. Miller was so good at singing!

「なんて」is used after a verb or adjective, as in ③, ④, and ⑤.「なんか」cannot be used in this case.

5.（1）～（さ）せる（emotional causative）

〈How to create forms〉

Vi.（emotion verb）＋（さ）せる

In addition to being used to express making someone else do something, the causative form「～（さ）せる」is also used to describe evoking an emotion. In this case, the verb used is an intransitive verb that indicates emotion, such as「泣く、びっくりする、楽しむ or 驚く」(cry, be surprised, enjoy, be startled, etc.), and the person in whom the emotion is provoked is indicated by「を」:

① 殴って、弟を泣かせたことがある。

I sometimes hit my younger brother and made him cry.

② テストで100点を取って、母をびっくりさせた。

I surprised my mother by scoring 100 points in the test.

Ref: 「～（さ）せる（causative）」: 部長は加藤さんを大阪へ出張させます。

（☞『みんなの日本語初級Ⅱ』Lesson 48）

5.（2）～（さ）せられる・～される（passive of emotional causative）

〈How to create forms〉

Vi.＋（さ）せられる／される

The emotional causative can also be used in the passive:

① 何度買っても宝くじが当たらず、がっかりさせられた。

I was disappointed when I never won anything in the lottery, no matter how many times I bought tickets.

② 子どもが書いた作文はすばらしく、感心させられた。

The composition the child wrote was excellent; I was impressed.

This usage indicates that the emotion (of surprise, sadness, disappointment, admiration, etc.) is strongly evoked.

Ref: 「～（さ）せる（causative）」: 部長は加藤さんを大阪へ出張させます。

(☞『みんなの日本語初級Ⅱ』Lesson 48)

「～（ら）れる（passive）」: わたしは先生に褒められました。

(☞『みんなの日本語初級Ⅱ』Lesson 37)

「～（さ）せられる（causative-passive）」: 太郎君は先生に掃除をさせられました。

(☞『みんなの日本語中級Ⅰ』Lesson 4)

6. …なら、…

V	plain form		+ なら
いA	plain form		
なA	plain form		
N	ーだ		

「XならY」 is used to recommend or ask about Y when the listener is thinking of doing X or is in a state of X. X can be a noun, verb or adjective.

「なら」 is appended to the plain form, but when X ends in a なA or a noun, the form なA/noun ＋なら is used:

① パソコンを買いたいんですが。

…パソコンならパワー電気のがいいですよ。 (☞『みんなの日本語初級Ⅱ』Lesson 35)

② ワインを買うなら、あの酒屋に安くておいしいものがあるよ。

If it's wine you're buying, that off-licence has some that are good and cheap.

③ 日曜大工でいすを作るなら、まず材料に良い木を選ばなくてはいけません。

If you're going to make a chair by yourself, you have to start by choosing some good wood as a material.

④ 頭が痛いなら、この薬を飲むといいですよ。

If you've got a headache, you should take some of this medicine, you know.

⑤ 大学院への進学のことを相談するなら、どの先生がいいかな。

If I'm going to get some advice about going on a postgraduate course, I wonder which professor I should talk to?

読む・書く

～てくれ

(1)「Vてくれ」is used when you instruct or request something indirectly. When speaking directly, the form「～てください」is used:

① 田中さんはお母さんに「7時に起こしてください」と言いました。

Mr. Tanaka said to his mother, "Please wake me up at seven o'clock."

→ 田中さんはお母さんに何と言いましたか。

What did Mr. Tanaka say to his mother?

…7時に起こしてくれと言いました。

He asked her to wake him up at seven o'clock.

(2) Note that Vてくれ is mainly used by men when asking someone junior to do something and sounds a little rough:

② 部長：田中君、この資料をコピーして来てくれ。

Department Manager: Tanaka, go and copy these materials, please.

Lesson 8

1.（1）（2） ～あいだ、…・～あいだに、…

Vている Nの	}	+	{ あいだ あいだに

（1）「Xあいだ、Y」shows that, in a situation where both X and Y continue for a certain period of time, Y is going on at the same time as X:

① 電車に乗っているあいだ、本を読んでいた。

While on the train, I was reading a book.

② 夏休みのあいだ、ずっと国に帰っていた。

I was back in my home country for the whole of the summer holidays.

（2）「Xあいだに、Y」shows that an isolated event (Y) takes place in a situation where X is going on:

③ 食事に出かけているあいだに、部屋に泥棒が入った。

A burglar broke into my room while I was out to eat.

④ 旅行のあいだに、アパートに泥棒が入った。

A burglar broke into our flat while we were away on holiday.

Ref: 「あいだ（position）」: 郵便局は銀行と本屋のあいだ（間）にあります。

（☞『みんなの日本語初級Ⅰ』Lesson 10）

2.（1）（2） ～まで、…・～までに、…

N V dic. -form	}	+	{ まで までに

（1）In「XまでY」, X indicates the final limit of Y, where Y is a continuing action or situation:

① 3時までここにいます。

② 毎日9時から5時まで働きます。 （☞『みんなの日本語初級Ⅰ』Lesson 4）

X can be an event instead of a time:

③ 先生が来るまで、ここで待っていましょう。

Let's wait here until our teacher comes.

(2) In「X までに Y」, X is also a limit, but Y is not a continuing action or situation; it is a one-off event. It shows that Y occurs before X:

④ 3時までに帰ります。 (☞『みんなの日本語初級 I』Lesson 17)

⑤ 先生が来るまでに、掃除を終わらせた。

I got the cleaning done before our teacher arrived.

3. ～た～ (noun modifier)

V た -form + N

(1) When a ている -form verb indicating a situation that has arisen as a result of the completion of an action or change is used to modify a noun, the ている -form can be replaced by the た -form:

① 田中さんは眼鏡をかけています。→ 眼鏡をかけた田中さん

Mr. Tanaka is wearing spectacles. → The spectacle-wearing Mr. Tanaka

② 線が曲がっている。→ 曲がった線 The line is curved. → The curved line

(2) However, when a noun is modified by a ている -form verb that indicates an ongoing action, the meaning changes if the ている -form is replaced by the た -form:

③ 山下さんは本を読んでいます。 ≠ 本を読んだ山下さん

Mr. Yamashita is reading a book. Mr. Yamashita, who read a book

④ 東京電気で働いている友達 ≠ 東京電気で働いた友達

My friend, who works at Tokyo Electric My friend, who worked at Tokyo Electric

Ref: 「ている (showing the state of an effect)」: 窓が割れています。

(☞『みんなの日本語初級 II』Lesson 29)

4. ～によって…

N + によって

In「X によって Y」, Y indicates that something varies depending on the type of X. The predicate of Y comes usually with「違う」(differs),「変わる」(changes),「さまざまだ」(varies), etc.:

① 好きな食べ物は人によって違う。 Everyone likes different things to eat.

② 季節によって景色が変わる。 The scenery changes according to the season.

5. ～たまま、…・ ～のまま、…

Vた -form
Nの } **＋ まま**

「VたままY／NのままY」indicates doing Y in the state pertaining after an action (V) has taken place, or indicated by a noun (N). It is used in cases where Y is not usually done in the situation described:

① 眼鏡をかけたまま、おふろに入った。　I got into the bath with my glasses on.

② 昨夜の地震にはびっくりして、下着のまま、外に出た。

I was so startled by last night's earthquake that I ran out in my underwear.

6. …からだ（cause / reason）

（1）S（plain form）＋ からだ

（2）S（plain form）＋ のは、S（plain form）＋ からだ

(1) This is a way of stating the cause of, or reason for, an event. It is used when replying to an inquiry as to the reason for something:

① どうして医者になりたいんですか。 Why do you want to become a doctor?

…医者は人を助けるすばらしい仕事だからです。

Because being a doctor is a wonderful job in which you help people.

(2) When stating a result first, and then the reason for it, the sentence becomes「…(plain form) ＋ のは、…(plain form) ＋ からだ」:

② 急にドアが開いたのは、だれかがボタンを押したからだ。

The reason why the door suddenly opened was that someone pressed the button.

Although, like「から」,「…ので」indicates a reason, it cannot be used in this way, because one cannot say,「…のでだ／…のでです」.

Ref: 「…から（reason: joins two sentences together）」:

時間がありませんから、新聞を読みません。

（☞『みんなの日本語初級Ⅰ』Lesson 9）

話す・聞く

髪／目／形（hair / eyes / shape）をしている

This is an expression used to describe a visual characteristic of a person or thing:

① リンリンちゃんは長い髪をしています。　Little Rin-Rin has long hair.

② この人形は大きい目をしています。　This doll has big eyes.

③ このパンは帽子みたいな形をしている。　This loaf is shaped like a hat.

Lesson 9

1. お～~~ます~~です

This is the respectful form of the「～している」form of a verb. It is used as a respectful way of describing an ongoing action or the state remaining as the result of an action:

① 何をお読みですか。　May I ask what you are reading?
　= 何を読んでいますか。　What are you reading?

② いい時計をお持ちですね。　Excuse me for saying so, but you have a nice watch.
　= いい時計を持っていますね。　You have a nice watch.

With a stative verb, it is used as a way of respectfully describing the current situation:

③ 時間がおありですか。　Excuse me, but are you free at the moment?
　=時間がありますか。　Are you free?

Also, with verbs that usually indicate arriving and departing, depending on the situation, it can be used as a respectful form of the verb, past or future:

④ 部長は何時にお着きですか。　What time will the Department Manager be arriving? = 部長は何時に着きますか。　What time will the Department Manager be arriving?

⑤ (夕方、隣の家の人に会って) 今、お帰りですか。
　[*On seeing a neighbor in the evening*] Have you just got home?
　=今、帰りましたか。　Have you just got home?

With the following verbs, it takes a special form:

⑥ 行く・いる・来る (go/be/come) → おいでです
　来る (come) → お越しです・お見えです
　食べる (eat) → お召し上がりです
　着る (wear) → お召しです
　寝る (sleep) → お休みです
　住んでいる (live) → お住まいです
　知っている (know) → ご存じです

2. ～てもかまわない

Vて-form
いA　ー~~い~~ → くて
なA
N　} ＋ で
} ＋ もかまわない

「～てもかまわない」indicates allowing or giving permission to do something. In an interrogative sentence, it is used for asking permission to do something. Although it means the same as「～てもいい」, it is more formal:

① ここに座(すわ)ってもかまいませんか。　May I sit here, please?

② 間(ま)に合(あ)わなかったら、あしたでもかまいません。

If you run out of time today, tomorrow will be acceptable.

Ref: 「～てもいい（permission）」: 写真(しゃしん)を撮(と)ってもいいです。

（☞『みんなの日本語初級Ⅰ』Lesson 15）

3. …ほど～ない・…ほどではない（comparison）

（1）N
V plain form
} ほど { **いA　ー~~い~~ → く ＋ ない**
なA　ー~~だ~~ → ではない

（2）N
V plain form
} ほどではない

（1）「AはBほどXではない」indicates that both A and B are X, but that A is less so than B :

① 中国(ちゅうごく)は日本(にほん)より広(ひろ)いが、ロシアほど広(ひろ)くはない。

China is bigger than Japan but not as big as Russia.

② 八ヶ岳(やつがたけ)は有名(ゆうめい)な山(やま)だが、富士山(ふじさん)ほど有名(ゆうめい)ではない。

Yatsugatake is a well-known mountain, but not as famous as Mt. Fuji.

③ 田中先生(たなかせんせい)は厳(きび)しいですか。　Is Mr. Tanaka strict?

…ええ、でも、鈴木先生(すずきせんせい)ほど厳(きび)しくないですよ。

Yes, but not as strict as Mr. Suzuki.

A plain-form verb can be used for「B」, as in「思(おも)ったほど」or「考(かんが)えていたほど」.

④ このレストランは人気(にんき)があるそうだが、料理(りょうり)は思(おも)ったほどおいしくなかった。

This restaurant is said to be popular, but the food was not as good as I thought it would be.

(2) X can be omitted:

⑤ 10月に入って少し寒くなったが、まだコートを着るほどではない。

It's become a little colder now we're into October, but not enough to have to wear a coat.

4. ～ほど～はない／いない（comparison）

Nほど { いA / なA ーな } N＋はない／いない

「XほどYはない／いない」means that X is the pinnacle of whatever is indicated by Y:

① スポーツのあとに飲むビールほどおいしいものはない。

There's nothing so delicious as a beer drunk after sport.

② 田中さんほど仕事がよくできる人はいません。

Nobody can do the job as well as Mr. Tanaka.

③ この島で見る星ほど美しいものはありません。

There's nothing so beautiful as the stars seen from this island.

④ 田中先生ほど親切で熱心な先生はいない。

There are no other teachers as kind and enthusiastic as Mr. Tanaka.

⑤ アジアで『ドラえもん』ほどよく知られている漫画はありません。

There are no other comics as well known in Asia as 'Doraemon.'

5. …ため［に］、…・…ためだ（cause / reason）

S（plain form） / いA / なA ーな / Nの } ＋ { ため ［に］ / ためだ

In「Xために、Y」, X is a cause or reason, and Y is what happened. This expression is used in writing, and is more formal than「から」or「ので」. When the result is stated first and the cause or reason is given as a predicate, the construction becomes「Y（の）はXためだ」:

① 大雪が降ったために、空港が使えなくなりました。

Because a lot of snow fell, the airport became unusable.

② 空港が使えなくなったのは、大雪が降ったためです。

The reason why the airport became unusable was that a lot of snow fell.

6. ～たら／～ば、…た（counterfactual usage）

Vたら／Vば、…た

いA　ー~~い~~ → かったら／けれぱ、
なA　＋ だったら／なら、 } **…た**

This expression is used when hypothesizing about what would have happened if an event that had not occurred had actually occurred. The sentence ends with a conjectural expression,「のに」, etc.:

① もし昨日雨が降っていたら、買い物には出かけなかっただろう。

I probably wouldn't have gone shopping yesterday if it had rained.

② お金があれば、このパソコンが買えたのに。

I could have bought that personal computer if only I had had the money.

③ この間見たパソコン、買ったんですか。

Did you buy that personal computer that you were looking at the other day?

…いいえ、もう少し安ければ、買ったんですが……。

No, if it had been a bit cheaper, I'd have bought it, but....

Ref: 「～たら（hypothetical）」: お金があったら、旅行します。

「～たら（something that will definitely happen in the future）」:

10時になったら、出かけましょう。 （☞『みんなの日本語初級Ⅰ』Lesson 25）

「～ば（conditional）」: ボタンを押せば、窓が開きます。

（☞『みんなの日本語初級Ⅱ』Lesson 35）

Lesson 10

1.（1）…はずだ

V いA	plain form	+ はずだ
なA	plain form ーだ → な	
N	plain form ーだ → の	

「…はずだ」shows that the speaker strongly believes something to be true, based on calculation, prior knowledge or logic:

① 飛行機で東京まで１時間だ。２時に大阪を出発すれば３時には着くはずだ。

It takes one hour to get to Tokyo by air. If we leave Osaka at two, we should arrive at three.

② 薬を飲んだから、もう熱は下がるはずだ。

I took the medicine, so my temperature should be coming down already.

③ 子どもが８人もいたから、生活は楽ではなかったはずだ。

He had eight children, so his life couldn't have been easy.

「はず」is used like a noun in expressions such as「はずなのに」,「はずの」and「そのはず」:

④ 山田さんは来ますか。　Is Mr. Yamada coming?

…はい、そのはずです。　Yes, he's supposed to.

Ref: 「…はずだ」:

ミラーさんは今日来るでしょうか。

…来るはずですよ。昨日電話がありましたから。

（☞『みんなの日本語初級Ⅱ』Lesson 46）

1.（2）…はずが／はない

V / いA	plain form	+ はずが／はない
なA	plain form ーだ → な	
N	plain form ーだ → の	

「はずがない／はずはない」, the negative form of「はずだ」, means ‘impossible,’ or ‘out of the question.’ It is used for strongly denying something, based on sound reasoning:

① あんなに練習したんだから、今日の試合は負けるはずがない。

They've practiced so hard, there's no way they can lose today's match.

② 人気がある映画なのだから、おもしろくないはずはありません。

It's a popular film, so it can't possibly be dull.

③ 階段の前に1週間前から赤い自転車が置いてある。ワットさんも赤い自転車を持っているが、今修理に出してある。だからこの自転車はワットさんの自転車のはずがない。

Someone left a red bicycle in front of the steps, and it's been there for a week. Although Mr. Watt owns a red bicycle, it's at the repair shop, so the abandoned bicycle cannot be his.

When strongly denying what someone has said, implying that it is not true, the expression「そんなはずはない」is used:

④ かぎがかかっていなかったよ。　The door wasn't locked, you know.

…そんなはずはありません。　That can't be true!

1.（3）…はずだった

V / いA	plain form	+ はずだった
なA	plain form ーだ → な	
N	plain form ーだ → の	

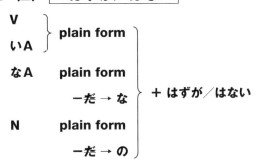

「…はずだった」, the past form of「…はずだ」, indicates that the speaker thinks that something had been bound to happen. It is used most often when a result has turned out to be different from what had been expected:

① 旅行に行くはずだった。しかし、病気で行けなくなった。

I was supposed to go on a trip, but I fell ill and couldn't go.

② パーティーには出ないはずだったが、部長が都合が悪くなったので、わたしが出席することになった。

I wasn't supposed to be going to the party, but the Department Manager couldn't make it, so I had to go instead.

Ref: 「…はずだ」:

ミラーさんは今日来るでしょうか。

…来るはずですよ。昨日電話がありましたから。

(☞『みんなの日本語初級Ⅱ』Lesson 46)

2. …ことが／もある

V dic. -form
Vない -form　ーない
いA
なA　ーな
Nの
} **＋ ことが／もある**

(1)「…ことがある・こともある」means that an event occasionally happens or a situation sometimes arises:

① 8月はいい天気が続くが、ときどき大雨が降ること {が／も} ある。

August is going to be mainly fine, but it will occasionally rain heavily.

② 母の料理はいつもおいしいが、ときどきおいしくないこと {が／も} ある。

My mother's cooking usually tastes very good, but sometimes it doesn't.

③ このスーパーはほとんど休みがないが、たまに休みのこと {が／も} ある。

This supermarket hardly ever closes, but occasionally it does.

(2)「…ことがある」and「こともある」are mostly used with the same meaning:

④ このエレベーターは古いから、たまに止まること {が／も} ある。

This lift is old, so it sometimes stops.

⑤ 彼女の電話はいつも長いが、たまには短いこと {が／も} ある。

Her phone calls usually take a long time, but sometimes they are short.

⑥ うちの子どもたちはとても元気だが、1年に何度か熱を出すこと {が／も} ある。

Our children are very healthy, but they do run a temperature several times a year.

Ref: 「V た -form + ことがある (experience)」:

わたしはパリに行ったことがあります。 (☞『みんなの日本語初級 I』Lesson 19)

3. ～た結果、…・～の結果、…

V た -form } + **結果 (result)、…**
N の

This shows that the occurrence of an action (～) led to a subsequent event (…) taking place. It is mainly used in writing, but it is also often used on the TV or radio news:

① {調査した／調査の} 結果、この町の人口が減ってきていることがわかりました。

The investigation showed that the population of this town is shrinking.

② 両親と {話し合った／の話し合いの} 結果、アメリカに留学することに決めました。

After discussing it with my parents, I decided to go to college in the U.S.

4. (1) ～出す (compound verbs)

「V ます -form + 出す」 means that the action indicated by V commences, e.g., 泣き出す (burst out crying), (雨が) 降り出す (begin to rain), 動き出す (start to move), 歩き出す (begin walking), 読み出す (start reading), 歌い出す (begin singing) and 話し出す (start talking):

① 急に雨が降り出した。Suddenly it began to rain.

「V ます -form + 出す」 cannot be used for inviting or requesting someone to do something:

② 先生がいらっしゃったら、{○食べ始めましょう／×食べ出しましょう}。(invitation)

Let's start eating when our teacher gets here.

③ 本を {○読み始めてください／×読み出してください}。(request)

Please start reading your books.

4．(2) ～始める・～終わる・～続ける（compound verbs）

These show V beginning, ending and continuing:

① 雨は3時間くらい続きましたが、電話がかかってきたのは、{○雨が降り始めた／×雨が降った} ときでした。

The rain fell for about three hours, but it was when it started that we received the phone call.

② 宿題の作文を {○書き終わる／×書く} 前に、友達が遊びに来た。

My friends came round to see me before I had finished writing my homework composition.

③ 5分間走り続けてください。　Please keep running for about five minutes.

4．(3) ～忘れる・～合う・～換える（compound verbs）

(1)「V ます -form ＋忘れる」means to forget to do V:

① 今日の料理は塩を入れ忘れたので、おいしくない。

The food tastes bland today because I forgot to put in any salt.

(2)「V ます -form ＋合う」means that several people or things do V with each other:

② 困ったときこそ助け合うことが大切だ。

When we're in trouble is the very time when it is important to help each other.

(3)「V ます -form ＋ 換える」means to change something by doing V, or to do V differently:

③ 部屋の空気を入れ換えた。　I let some fresh air into the room.

④ 電車からバスに乗り換えた。　I changed from the train to a bus.

読む・書く

…ということになる

「…ということになる」is used to sum up several items of information and state the implications (…) of a situation:

① 申し込む学生が10人以上にならなければ、この旅行は中止ということになる。

Unless at least ten students apply, the trip will be cancelled.

② 今夜カレーを食べれば、3日続けてカレーを食べたということになる。

If we have curry tonight, we will have had it three days in a row.

Lesson 11

1. ～てくる・～ていく（change）

(1)「～てくる」indicates arriving at a present situation through a process of change:

① だんだん春らしくなってきました。　Little by little, it became spring-like.

(2)「～ていく」indicates moving in the direction of a future change:

② これからは、日本で働く外国人が増えていくでしょう。

The number of non-Japanese nationals working in Japan will probably increase from now on.

Ref:「～てくる・～ていく（direction of motion）」: 兄が旅行から帰ってきた。

（☞『みんなの日本語中級Ⅰ』Lesson 6）

2. ～たら［どう］？

Vたら

(1) This expression is used when making a suggestion to someone by simply indicating a choice they could make.「～たらいかがですか」is a polite form of「～たらどう？」:

① A：今日は恋人の誕生日なんだ。　It's my girlfriend's birthday today.

B：電話でもかけて｛あげたらどう／あげたらいかがですか｝？

Why don't you call her or something?

(2)「～たらどう？」and「～たら？」are used when speaking to someone junior or someone with whom one is on familiar terms, such as a family member or friend:

② A：少し熱があるみたい…。　I think I've got a bit of a temperature.

B：薬を飲んで、今日は早く寝たら？

How about taking some medicine and going to bed early today?

3. …より…ほうが…（comparison）

V / いA } dic. -form
なA
N
} **より** {
V / いA } dic. -form
なA －な
Nの
} ＋ **ほうが…**

(1)「YよりXほうが…」is mainly used in answer to the question「XとYとではどちらが…ですか」(which is …, X or Y?), where「…」is a comparative:

① 北海道と東京とではどちらが寒いですか。

Which is colder, Hokkaido or Tokyo?

…○ 北海道のほうが寒いです。 Hokkaido is colder.

× 北海道は東京より寒いです。 Hokkaido is colder than Tokyo.

(2)「YよりXほうが…」can be used even when not replying to a question. The nuance is then, "You would probably expect Y to be more「…」than X, but actually the reverse is true."

② 今日は、北海道より東京のほうが気温が低かったです。

The temperature was lower in Tokyo than in Hokkaido today.

③ 漢字は見て覚えるより書いて覚えるほうが忘れにくいと思います。

I think it is harder to forget the kanji if you learn them by writing them than if you learn them just by looking at them.

④ パーティーの料理は少ないより多いほうがいいです。

At a party, it is better to have too much food than too little.

⑤ 子どもに食べさせる野菜は、値段が安いより安全なほうがいい。

It is better for vegetables given to children to eat to be safe rather than cheap.

Ref: 「～は～より (comparison)」: この車はあの車より大きいです。

「～がいちばん～ (the maximum of something indicated by an adjective)」:

日本料理［の中］で何がいちばんおいしいですか。

…てんぷらがいちばんおいしいです。 (☞『みんなの日本語初級 I』Lesson 12)

4. ～らしい

Nらしい

「N_1らしいN_2」indicates that N_2 possesses a typical quality or property of N_1:

① 山本さんの家はいかにも日本の家らしい家です。

Ms. Yamamoto's house is so typically Japanese.

② 春らしい色のバッグですね。 That bag is spring-like in color, isn't it?

③ これから試験を受ける会社へ行くときは学生らしい服を着て行ったほうがいいですよ。

When you go to the companies where you will be taking a test, it would be better to wear clothes that make you look like a student, you know.

「N らしい」can also be the predicate of a sentence:

④ 今日の田中さんの服は学生らしいね。

The clothes Mr. Tanaka is wearing today make him look like a student, don't they?

⑤ 文句を言うのはあなたらしくない。　It's not like you to complain.

5. …らしい (reported speech / conjecture)

V / いA	plain form	+ らしい
なA / N	plain form —だ	

(1)「…らしい」indicates that「…」is reported speech (information that has been read or heard):

① 新聞によると、昨日の朝中国で大きい地震があったらしい。

According to the newspaper, there was a large earthquake in China yesterday morning.

② 雑誌で見たんだけど、あの店のケーキはおいしいらしいよ。

I read it in a magazine, but that shop's cakes are apparently very good.

③ 先生の話では、試験の説明は全部英語らしい。

From what the teacher said, it would appear that the exam instructions are all in English.

(2)「…らしい」can also indicate that one thinks something is probably true (a conjecture) based on information read or heard:

④ パーティーが始まったらしい。会場の中からにぎやかな声が聞こえてくる。

It looks like the party has started. There are noisy voices coming from the hall.

⑤ 山田さんはずいぶんのどがかわいていたらしい。コップのビールを休まずに全部飲んでしまったよ。

Mr. Yamada seemed pretty thirsty. He drank his glass of beer in one go.

Ref:「N らしい (simile, illustration)」: 春らしい色のバッグですね。

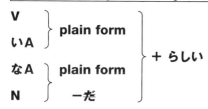

6. ～として

Nとして

In「～として」,「～」indicates a qualification, position or perspective:

① 会社の代表として、お客さんに新しい商品の説明をした。

I explained the new product to the customers on behalf of the company.

② 東京は、日本の首都として世界中に知られている。

Tokyo is known around the world as the capital of Japan.

7. (1) ～ず［に］…（attendant circumstances, means）

Vない-form ＋ず［に］…（but「～する」→「～せず」）

「～ず［に］…」indicates attendant circumstances or means. It is the same as「～ないで…」but is more in the written than in the spoken style:

① その男は先週の土曜日にこの店に来て、一言も話さず、酒を飲んでいた。

That guy came to this bar last Saturday and was drinking without saying a word.

② 急いでいたので、かぎを｛かけずに／かけないで｝出かけてしまった。

I was in such a hurry that I left without locking up. (attendant circumstances)

③ 辞書を｛使わずに／使わないで｝新聞が読めるようになりたい。

I'd like to be able to read a newspaper without using a dictionary. (means)

7. (2) ～ず、…（cause / reason, parataxis）

Vない-form ＋ず、…（but「～する」→「～せず」）

(1)「～ず、…」indicates a cause or reason. It is the same as「～なくて、…」but is used more in writing:

① 子どもの熱が｛下がらず／下がらなくて｝、心配しました。

The child's temperature didn't come down, so I was worried.

(2)「Xず、Y」can also be used to juxtapose clauses or phrases, as in「Xない。そして、Y。」(not X, but Y.):

② 田中さんは今月出張せず、来月出張することになりました。

Mr. Tanaka isn't going away on business this month; he is to go next month instead.

Ref: 「～なくて（cause and effect）」: 家族に会えなくて、寂しいです。

（☞『みんなの日本語初級Ⅱ』Lesson 39）

8. ～ている（experience / record, history）

(1) 「～ている」indicates a historical fact, experience, record or history. It is often used with an adverb expressing frequency or duration, such as「～回」(times), or「長い間」(for a long time):

① この寺は今まで２回火事で焼けている。　This temple has burnt down twice.

② 京都では長い間大きな地震が起こっていない。もうすぐ地震が来るかもしれない。

There haven't been any big earthquakes in Kyoto for a long time. There may be one soon.

(2) This type of「～ている」is used when the fact that a certain action has taken place in the past is relevant to the present situation:

③ 田中さんは高校のときアメリカに留学している。だから、英語の発音がきれいだ。

Mr. Tanaka studied in the U.S. when he was at high school. That's why his English pronunciation is so good.

Ref: 「～ている（ongoing action）」: ミラーさんは今電話をかけています。

（☞『みんなの日本語初級Ⅰ』Lesson 14）

「～ている（resultant state）」: サントスさんは結婚しています。

（☞『みんなの日本語初級Ⅰ』Lesson 15）

「～ている（habit）」: 毎朝ジョギングをしています。

（☞『みんなの日本語初級Ⅱ』Lesson 28）

「～ている（resultant state）」: 窓が割れています。（☞『みんなの日本語初級Ⅱ』Lesson 29）

話(はな)す・聞(き)く

～なんかどう？

「～なんか」is used when proffering suitable examples to the listener. It implies that there are other examples worth considering, and is used to avoid appearing to force one's own suggestion onto the listener:

① ［店(みせ)で］これなんかいかがでしょうか。　(*At a shop*) How about this one?

② A：次(つぎ)の会長(かいちょう)はだれがいいかな。

Who would be best for the next Chairman, I wonder?

B：田中(たなか)さんなんかいいと思(おも)うよ。　I think Mr. Tanaka might be a good choice.

「～などどうですか」means the same but is a little more formal.

11

Lesson 12

1. …もの／もんだから

V いA	plain form	+ もの／もんだから
なA N	plain form ーだ → な	

「…もの／もんだから」indicates the reason or cause of something:

① 急(いそ)いでいたものですから、かぎをかけるのを忘(わす)れてしまいました。

I was in a rush, so I went and forgot to lock up.

② とても安(やす)かったものだから、買(か)いすぎたんです。

It was very cheap, so I bought too much.

「X ものだから Y」is sometimes used when an undesirable event (Y) has occurred, to justify it, or give a reason for it in order to deny responsibility and exculpate oneself:

③ A：どうしてこんなに遅(おそ)くなったんですか。　Why are you so late?

B：すみません。出(で)かけようとしたら、電話(でんわ)がかかってきたものですから。

I'm sorry; the telephone rang when I was about to leave.

It is not appropriate to use「…ものだから」in the same way as「から」and「ので」to indicate an objective cause or reason:

④ この飛行機(ひこうき)は1時間(じかん)に300キロ飛(と)ぶ｛○から／○ので／×ものだから｝、3時間(じかん)あれば向(む)こうの空港(くうこう)に着(つ)く。

This aircraft flies at 300 km/hr, so we can get to our destination airport in three hours.

Ref: 「…から（reason）」：

どうして朝(あさ)、新聞(しんぶん)を読(よ)みませんか。…時間(じかん)がありませんから。

（☞『みんなの日本語初級 I』Lesson 9）

2.（1） ～（ら）れる（indirect passive（intransitive verb））

In addition to direct passive sentences, in which the object Y of the transitive verb V of the active sentence「X が（は）Y を V する」becomes the subject of the passive sentence, Japanese passive sentences also include ones which take the indirect object Y of the active sentence「Xが（は）YにVする」as their subject, and also ones which take the owner Y of the object Z of the transitive verb V of the active sentence「XがYのZをVする」as their subject:

① 先生はわたしを注意した。(を → が（は))

→ わたしは先生に注意された。

② 部長はわたしに仕事を頼んだ。(に → が（は))

→ わたしは部長に仕事を頼まれた。

③ 泥棒がわたしの財布を盗んだ。(の→が（は))

→ わたしは泥棒に財布を盗まれた。 (①～③☞『みんなの日本語初級Ⅱ』Lesson 37)

In Japanese, it is also possible to make a passive sentence from an intransitive verb sentence, i.e.,「Xが（は）Vする」. In this case, the person affected by the action X becomes the subject of the passive sentence, indicating that he or she has been adversely affected by (i.e., has been inconvenienced or harmed by) the action:

④ 昨日雨が降った。(intransitive verb)　It rained yesterday.

→ わたしは昨日雨に降られて、ぬれてしまった。(passive of intransitive verb)

I was rained on yesterday and got wet.

⑤ あなたがそこに立つと、前が見えません。(intransitive verb)

→ あなたにそこに立たれると、前が見えません。(passive of intransitive verb)

If you stand there, I can't see what's in front of me.

The owner of the subject of an intransitive verb can also become the subject of a passive sentence:

⑥ わたしの父が急に死んで、わたしは大学に行けなかった。(intransitive verb)

My father died suddenly, and I couldn't go to university.

→ わたしは父に急に死なれて、大学に行けなかった。

(passive of intransitive verb)

I was affected by my father's death, and I couldn't go to university.

2. (2) ～（ら）れる（indirect passive（transitive verb))

A transitive verb can also be used in a passive sentence indicating that its subject has been inconvenienced or harmed:

① こんなところに信号を作られて、車が渋滞するようになってしまった。

They went and put some signals in a place like this, and now the traffic gets jammed up.

② わたしの家の前にゴミを捨てられて困っています。

I've got a problem with rubbish being dumped in front of my house.

Ref: 「～（さ）せられる／～される（causative-passive）」:

太郎君は先生に掃除をさせられた。 (☞『みんなの日本語中級 I』Lesson 4)

3. ～たり～たり

Vたり

いA → ー~~い~~かったり

なA → ーだったり

N → ーだったり

(1)「～たり～たり」is used for giving approximately two suitable examples from among a number of actions:

① 休みの日は、洗濯をしたり、掃除をしたりします。(listing of actions)

(☞『みんなの日本語初級 I』Lesson 19)

(2) In the construction「V_1たりV_2たり」, V_1 and V_2 can be verbs with opposite meanings, to express the fact that V_1 and V_2 are occurring alternately:

② 映画を見ているとき笑ったり泣いたりしました。

While watching the film, I was by turns laughing and crying.

③ この廊下は人が通ると、電気がついたり消えたりします。

With people passing down this corridor, the lights are by turns switched on and off.

「～たり～たり」can also be connected to adjectives to show that a number of different types of something exist:

④ この店の食べ物は種類が多くて、甘かったり辛かったりします。

This restaurant has a lot of dishes on the menu, including both sweet ones and spicy ones.

4. ～っぱなし

Vます-form ＋ っぱなし

「～っぱなし」indicates the undesirably lengthy continuation of a situation that normally would be terminated promptly:

① 服が脱ぎっぱなしだ。片づけないから、部屋が汚い。

You just take your clothes off and leave them lying around. You don't put them away, so your room is untidy.

② こらっ。ドアが開けっぱなしだよ。早く閉めなさい。

Hey, you've left the door open. Hurry up and shut it.

Ref: 「～たまま、…・～のまま、…」：

眼鏡をかけたまま、おふろに入った。　　(☞『みんなの日本語中級Ⅰ』Lesson 8)

5．(1) …おかげで、…・…おかげだ

V / いA	plain form	+	おかげで / おかげだ
なA	plain form ーだ → な		
N	plain form ーだ → の		

「X おかげで、Y・X おかげだ」is used when a favorable result (Y) is produced by a particular cause (X)：

① 先生が手紙を書いてくださったおかげで、大きい病院で研修を受けられることになった。

Thanks to my teacher writing a letter, I was able to get a training place at a big hospital.

② 値段が安かったおかげで、たくさん買えました。

Thanks to the price being low, I was able to buy a lot.

③ 地図の説明が丁寧なおかげで、待ち合わせの場所がすぐにわかりました。

Because the map was explained to me so carefully, I was easily able to find the meeting place.

④ 皆様のおかげで、スピーチ大会で優勝することができました。

Thanks to everyone's support and encouragement, I was able to win the speech contest.

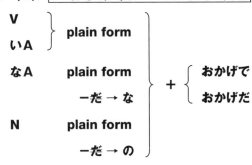

5. (2) …せいで、…・…せいだ

V / いA	plain form	+ せいで / せいだ
なA	plain form —だ → な	
N	plain form —だ → の	

Conversely, when an unfavorable result is produced,「…せいで・…せいだ」is used:

① 事故のせいで、授業に遅れてしまった。

I was late to the lesson because of the accident.

② {風邪薬を飲んでいる／風邪薬の} せいで、眠くなった。

Because {I had taken some cold medicine / of the cold medicine}, I felt sleepy.

話す・聞く

…みたいです (conjecture)

V / いA	plain form	+ みたいだ
なA / N	plain form —だ	

「…みたいです」indicates a guess from how a situation looks (e.g., something's external appearance):

① 電気が消えているね。隣の部屋は留守みたいだね。

The lights are out. It looks like the guys next door are out.

② 田中さんはお酒を飲んだみたいです。顔が赤いです。

It looks like Mr. Tanaka has been drinking. His face is red.

「…みたいです」means the same as「…ようだ」, which is used in writing or formal speech:

③ 資料が届いたようですので、事務室に取りに行ってまいります。

It looks like the documents have arrived, so I'll go to the office to get them.

Ref: 「…ようだ (guessing from a situation)」:

隣の部屋にだれかいるようです。 (☞『みんなの日本語初級Ⅱ』Lesson 47)

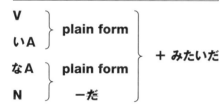

読む・書く

どちらかと言えば、～ほうだ

V いA	plain form	+ ほうだ
なA	plain form －だ → な	

「どちらかと言えば、Xほうだ」is used to indicate that a subject is strictly speaking, not completely X, but could be described as being X on the whole, without definitely committing oneself as to whether it is X or not:

① この辺りには高い店が多いのですが、この店はどちらかと言えば、安いほうです。
Most of the shops round here are expensive, but this one is on the cheaper side.

② わたしはどちらかと言えば、好き嫌いはあまりないほうだ。
I am someone who tends not to have strong likes and dislikes.

③ この町はわたしの国ではどちらかと言えば、にぎやかなほうです。
In my country, this town would be considered to lean toward the lively side.

④ 食事しながらお酒を飲みますか。 Do you drink alcohol with your meals?
…そうですね。いつもではありませんが、どちらかと言えば、飲むほうですね。
Let me see now. Not always, but I suppose I do tend to.

～ます／ませんように

(1)「～ますように／～ませんように」indicates wishing, hoping or praying that something will or will not happen. It is often used together with「どうか」or「どうぞ」when talking to oneself, or as a warning to someone else:

① 優しい人と結婚できますように。
I hope I can get married to someone nice.

② どうか大きい地震が起きませんように。
I hope there won't be any big earthquakes.

③ 先生もどうぞ風邪をひかれませんように。
I do hope you won't catch a cold, either, Sir.

Key Learning Points

Lesson	話す(はな)・聞く(き) (Speak and Listen)	読む(よ)・書く(か) (Read and Write)
Lesson 1	**お願い(ねが)があるんですが** **(There's a favor I'd like to ask you, if...)**	**畳(たたみ)** **(Tatami)**
Learning goals	Politely make a request one is hesitant about. Express gratitude.	Read a passage while noting where the history and merits of the things it discusses are described.
Grammar points	1. ～てもらえませんか・～ていただけませんか・～てもらえないでしょうか・～ていただけないでしょうか	2. ～のようだ・～のような～・～のように… 3. ～ことは／が／を 4. ～を～と言う(い) 5. ～という～ 6. いつ／どこ／何(なに)／だれ／どんなに～ても
Supplementary points	＊～じゃなくて、～	＊…のだ・…のではない ＊何人(なんにん)も、何回(なんかい)も、何枚(なんまい)も…
Lesson 2	**何(なん)のことですか** **(What does it mean?)**	**外来語(がいらいご)** **(Foreign Loanwords)**
Learning goals	Ask the meaning of an unfamiliar term, and check what to do.	Find examples and opinions.
Grammar points	1. (1) ～たら、～た (2) ～たら、～た 2. ～というのは～のことだ・～というのは…ということだ	5. ～みたいだ・～みたいな～・～みたいに…

	3．…という〜 4．…ように言う／注意する／伝える／頼む	
Supplementary points	＊〜ところ	
Lesson 3	**遅れそうなんです** **(It looks like I'm going to be late.)**	**時間よ、止まれ！** **(Time, stand still!)**
Learning goals	Explain a situation and apologize politely. Ask politely for something to be changed.	Guess what a text is about by looking at a graph.
Grammar points	1．〜(さ)せてもらえませんか・〜（さ）せていただけませんか・〜（さ）せてもらえないでしょうか・〜（さ）せていただけないでしょうか 2．(1) …ことにする (2) …ことにしている 3．(1) …ことになる (2) …ことになっている	4．〜てほしい・〜ないでほしい 5．(1) 〜そうな〜・〜そうに… (2) 〜なさそう (3) 〜そうもない
Supplementary points	＊〜たあと、…	
Lesson 4	**伝言、お願いできますか** **(Could I ask you to pass on a message?)**	**電話嫌い** **(Telephone-Shy)**
Learning goals	Receive a message, and ask someone to pass one on.	Read a passage while thinking about how feelings change.

	Leave a message on someone's voicemail.	
Grammar points	1．…ということだ 2．…の・…の？ 3．〜ちゃう・〜とく・〜てる	4．〜（さ）せられる・〜される 5．〜である 6．〜~~ます~~、〜~~ます~~、…・〜く~~て~~、〜く~~て~~、…［suspended form］ 7．(1) 〜（た）がる (2) 〜（た）がっている 8．…こと・…ということ
Supplementary points	＊〜の〜 ＊〜ましたら、…・〜まして、…	
Lesson 5	**どう行ったらいいでしょうか** **(How do I get to...?)**	**地図** **(Maps)**
Learning goals	Give and receive directions. Ask and tell the route to somewhere.	Read a passage while thinking about the reasons for something.
Grammar points	1．(1) あ〜・そ〜 (2) そ〜 2．…んじゃない？ 3．〜たところに／で	4．(1) 〜（よ）う［volitional form］とする (2) 〜（よ）う［volitional form］とする／しない 5．…のだろうか 6．〜との／での／からの／までの／への〜 7．…だろう・…だろうと思う
Supplementary points	＊…から、〜てください	＊が／の

Lesson 6	**行かせていただきたいんですが** **(I would like to be allowed to go....)**	**メンタルトレーニング** **(Mental Training)**
Learning goals	Announce that one wishes to ask for permission to do something. Obtain permission by negotiating.	Read a passage while thinking about what「こそあど」indicate.
Grammar points	1．(1) …て…・…って… (2) ～って…	2．(1) ～つもりはない (2) ～つもりだった (3) ～たつもり・～ているつもり 3．～てばかりいる・～ばかり～ている 4．…とか… 5．～てくる 6．～てくる・～ていく
Supplementary points		＊こ～
Lesson 7	**楽しみにしてます・遠慮させてください** **(I'm looking forward to it. Please forgive me for not ....)**	**まんじゅう、怖い** **(Scared of Bean-Jam Buns!)**
Learning goals	Gladly accept an invitation. Decline an invitation politely, explaining why.	Read a passage while noting who is speaking.
Grammar points	1．(1) ～なくてはならない／いけない・～なくてもかまわない	4．(1) ～なんか… (2) …なんて… 5．(1) ～（さ）せる

	(2) 〜なくちゃ／〜なきゃ［いけない］ 2．…だけだ・［ただ］…だけでいい 3．…かな	(2) 〜（さ）せられる・〜される 6．…なら、…
Supplementary points		＊〜てくれ
Lesson 8	**迷子（まいご）になっちゃったんです** **(I've lost my way!)**	**科学者（かがくしゃ）ってどう見（み）える？** **(What do you think of scientists?)**
Learning goals	Explain the circumstances of people, things, etc., in detail.	Find the answer to the question posed in the title. Read a passage while thinking about how each sentence relates to the ones before and after it.
Grammar points	1．(1) 〜あいだ、… (2) 〜あいだに、… 2．(1) 〜まで、… (2) 〜までに、… 3．〜た〜	4．〜によって… 5．〜たまま、…・〜のまま、… 6．…からだ
Supplementary points	＊髪（かみ）／目（め）／形（かたち）　をしている	
Lesson 9	**どこが違（ちが）うんですか** **(What's the difference?)**	**カラオケ** **(Karaoke)**
Learning goals	Communicate one's wishes and conditions about something one wants to buy. Compare differences and choose what one wants to buy.	Grasp the facts accurately. Understand what the writer thinks.

Grammar points	1．お　～~~ます~~　です 2．～てもかまわない 3．…ほど～ない・…ほどではない	4．～ほど～はない／いない 5．…ため［に］、…・…ためだ 6．～たら／～ば、…た
Lesson 10	**そんなはずはありません** **(That can't be true.)**	**記憶型(きおくがた)と注意型(ちゅういがた)** **(Memory-Type and Attention-Type)**
Learning goals	Respond calmly when misunderstood.	Read while looking for differences. Understand conclusions.
Grammar points	1．(1) …はずだ (2) …はずが／はない (3) …はずだった	2．…ことが／もある 3．～た結果(けっか)、…・～の結果(けっか)、… 4．(1) ～出(だ)す (2) ～始(はじ)める・～終(お)わる・～続(つづ)ける (3) ～忘(わす)れる・～合(あ)う・～換(か)える
Supplementary points		＊…ということになる
Lesson 11	**お勧(すす)めのところ、ありませんか** **(Is there anywhere you could recommend?)**	**白川郷(しらかわごう)の黄金伝説(おうごんでんせつ)** **(The Legend of the Shirakawa-go Gold)**
Learning goals	Make and receive suggestions.	Guess what the passage is about by looking at the photograph. Understand why the legend of the gold arose.
Grammar points	1．～てくる・～ていく 2．～たら［どう］？	5．…らしい 6．～として

	3. …より…ほうが… 4. ～らしい	7. (1) ～ず［に］… (2) ～ず、… 8. …ている
Supplementary points	＊～なんかどう？	
Lesson 12	**ご迷惑をかけてすみませんでした** **(I'm sorry to have been a nuisance.)**	**【座談会】 日本で暮らす** **(Round-Table Discussion: Living in Japan)**
Learning goals	Apologize after being complained about. Explain the circumstances.	Read while comparing differences in opinion.
Grammar points	1. …もの／もんだから 2. (1) ～（ら）れる (2) ～（ら）れる	3. ～たり～たり 4. ～っぱなし 5. (1) …おかげで、…・…おかげだ (2) …せいで、…・…せいだ
Supplementary points	＊…みたいです	＊どちらかと言えば、～ほうだ ＊～ます／ませんように

文法担当 Grammar
庵功雄（Iori Isao）　高梨信乃（Takanashi Shino）　中西久実子（Nakanishi Kumiko）
前田直子（Maeda Naoko）

執筆協力 Contributors
亀山稔史（Kameyama Toshifumi）　澤田幸子（Sawada Sachiko）　新内康子（Shin'uchi Koko）
関正昭（Seki Masaaki）　田中よね（Tanaka Yone）　鶴尾能子（Tsuruo Yoshiko）
藤嵜政子（Fujisaki Masako）　牧野昭子（Makino Akiko）　茂木真理（Motegi Mari）

編集協力 Editorial advisor
石沢弘子（Ishizawa Hiroko）

英語翻訳 English translator
John H. Loftus

イラスト Illustrator
佐藤夏枝（Sato Natsue）

本文レイアウト Layout designer
山田武（Yamada Takeshi）

編集担当 Editors
井上隆朗（Inoue Takao）　Nicholas McNeill

みんなの日本語（にほんご）　中級（ちゅうきゅう）Ⅰ
翻訳（ほんやく）・文法解説（ぶんぽうかいせつ）　英語版（えいごばん）

2009年6月1日　初版第1刷発行
2020年11月26日　第11刷発行

編著者　スリーエーネットワーク
発行者　藤嵜政子
発　行　株式会社　スリーエーネットワーク
〒102-0083 東京都千代田区麹町3丁目4番
トラスティ麹町ビル 2F
電話　営業　03（5275）2722
編集　03（5275）2726
https://www.3anet.co.jp/
印　刷　倉敷印刷株式会社

ISBN978-4-88319-492-6　C0081